SHAYS' REBELLION AND THE CONSTITUTION IN AMERICAN HISTORY

Mary E. Hull

Enslow Publishers, Inc.

40 Industrial Road   PO Box 38
Box 398   Aldershot
Berkeley Heights, NJ 07922   Hants GU12 6BP
USA   UK

http://www.enslow.com

Library of Congress Cataloging-in-Publication Data

Hull, Mary.
    Shays' Rebellion and the Constitution in American history / Mary E. Hull.
        p. cm. — (In American history)
    Includes bibliographical references (p.) and index.
    SUMMARY: Describes the attempted revolt of Massachusetts farmers and yeomen which revealed the instability of the Articles of Confederation and the need for a stronger Constitution.
    ISBN 0-7660-1418-5
    1. Shays' Rebellion, 1786–1787 Juvenile literature. 2. Shays' Rebellion, 1786–1787—Influence Juvenile literature. 3. Constitutional history—United States—18th century Juvenile literature. [1. Shays' Rebellion, 1786–1787. 2. Constitutional history—United States.] I. Title. II. Series.
    F69 .H94 2000
    974.4'03—dc21   99-37012
                                                       CIP

CUR2

Printed in the United States of America

10 9 8 7 6 5 4 3 2 1

To Our Readers: All Internet addresses in this book were active and appropriate when we went to press. Any comments or suggestions can be sent by e-mail to Comments@enslow.com or to the address on the back cover.

Illustration Credits: Enslow Publishers, Inc., pp. 30, 82; Mary Hull, pp. 10, 103; C. O. Parmenter, *History of Pelham, Massachusetts* (Amherst: Carpenter and Morehouse, 1898), pp. 61, 62, 63, 83; The Jones Library, Amherst, p. 89; National Portrait Gallery, Smithsonian Institution, p. 9; Historical Society of Pennsylvania, p. 75; Massachusetts Historical Society, pp. 23, 66; Reproduced from the *Dictionary of American Portraits*, Published by Dover Publications, Inc., in 1967, pp. 56, 71; John Grafton, *The American Revolution: A Picture Sourcebook* (New York: Dover Publications, Inc., 1975), pp. 14, 95, 98; Library of Congress, pp. 19, 53, 100; Springfield Armory National Historic Site, p. 6; Massachusetts State Archives, p. 91; M. C. Coolidge, *History of Pelham* (Hudson, Mass.: Powell Press, 1848), pp. 86, 92; *Massachusetts Magazine*, 1793, p. 42; G. R. Minot, *The History of the Insurrections in Massachusetts in 1786*, p. 16.

Cover Illustration: C. O. Parmenter, *History of Pelham, Massachusetts* (Amherst: Carpenter and Morehouse, 1898); Library of Congress; National Portrait Gallery, Smithsonian Institution; Mabel Cook Coolidge, *History of Pelham* (Hudson, Mass.: Powell Press, 1848).

★ CONTENTS ★

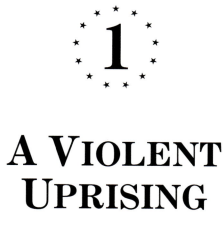

A VIOLENT UPRISING

During the cold, snowy January of 1787, farmers from the hills and valleys of western Massachusetts prepared to leave the warmth and comfort of their homes and families to fight a civil war. They readied their muskets and filled the powder horns they had used just a few years earlier while fighting for independence from England in the American Revolution. Saying good-bye to their families, they marched toward Springfield, Massachusetts, where they would meet like-minded men and launch an attack on their own government. These men, known as Regulators, marched through the snow with the conviction that what they were doing was necessary. They were convinced that their farms and homes and the livelihood of their families depended on their actions.

These farmers-turned-rebels were planning to launch an attack on the federal arsenal at Springfield, which had been built in 1778 to house military supplies for the nation. The arsenal contained cannons, seven thousand muskets, thirteen hundred barrels of gunpowder, and piles of cannon shot.[1] The Regulators

The Springfield arsenal, built in 1778, would be the target of the Regulators' attack.

planned to seize the guns and ammunition. Then they would march to Boston, where they hoped to overthrow the state government and free themselves from the tyranny they had experienced for nearly a decade.

Life in rural Massachusetts after the revolution had been difficult. In the decade following the war, a financial crisis plagued Massachusetts. A poor economy and inflation caused paper currency to be devalued to the point where it was worth only a fraction of its face value.

This financial crisis hit farmers especially hard, and the policies of the Massachusetts government had made the situation worse. Attempting to pay off its huge war debt, Massachusetts had placed heavy taxes on land, and the state had demanded that these taxes be paid in cash. Rural farmers, laborers, and craftsmen, also known as yeomen, made enough to survive on, but little, if any, extra. They had little cash on hand, and what wealth they might have was tied up in land or goods. Many yeomen had spent some time away from home fighting in the revolution. However, the currency with which they had been paid for their military service was now worth far less than its face value. As a result, they did not have much money.

Those who could not pay their taxes or their debts risked losing their farms and livestock to creditors. At that time, debt was considered a punishable crime. Some debtors had even been thrown into debtor's prison, where they faced starvation and disease.

In contrast, the wealthier citizens of Massachusetts, such as merchants, shopkeepers, and traders, who lived a commercial lifestyle, were better able to pay their taxes. Their money was often tied up in merchandise rather than land alone. Thus they did not have to pay the steep taxes that were placed on landowners. Merchants were also well represented in the Massachusetts government. They had a lot of power and influence in politics. For a long time, the back-country farmers had accused the government of favoring merchants and their interests. They did not believe the interests of yeomen were being considered.

Throughout the 1780s, yeomen had banded together and petitioned the government for relief. They lobbied for policies that would help them, such as reform of the debtor courts and lower court fees.

They wanted more time to pay their debts and taxes, and they wanted to be able to pay in goods, such as wool or wheat, as they had been allowed to do in previous years. Yeomen worked for many years to achieve some kind of solution to their financial problems. But their efforts to petition the legislature had gained them little. A few years after the revolution, they were no better off than they had been before the long war.

Gradually, yeomen began to abandon peaceful means of protest. More yeomen became convinced that action, even if it included violence, was the only way to show the government that they meant business. If their government would not allow them any way to improve their welfare, then they were not going to obey that government.

One of the yeomen who believed in taking action to improve the situation was Daniel Shays, a farmer from Pelham, Massachusetts. Shays had risen through the ranks of the yeoman Regulators, formed out of the old Revolutionary War militias. He had become a captain. His signature had appeared on several letters written by the Regulators, and people in Boston had begun to associate the Regulator movement with him. Soon people were calling all Regulators "Shaysites" because they thought Shays was their leader. Actually, the Regulators had no single leader. Those who had volunteered for the Regulator cause were loosely organized under seventeen different captains, of whom Shays was only one. But Massachusetts government officials, anxious to identify the leaders of the

Daniel Shays (left) and Job Shattuck were two of the best known leaders of the Regulator movement.

Regulators, latched onto Shays' name and continued to believe he was the general behind the movement.

After angry yeomen organized as Regulators, they held demonstrations against the government of Massachusetts. Their chief target consisted of the courts. Yeomen hated debtor courts, where indebted farmers were prosecuted by shopkeepers who had loaned them money or provided them with goods on credit, and then forced them to surrender their livestock, land, or other goods as payment for their debt. In addition, farmers had to pay the high court fees and lawyers' fees each time they were taken to court. A

The yeomen tried appealing to local government leaders for help in their situation. This is the town hall in Pelham, Massachusetts, as it looks today. At the time of the rebellion, it was both a town hall and a church that was attended by Daniel Shays.

debt of one pound (a unit of currency, like the dollar) could end up costing a farmer four times as much after he paid all court costs.

Since they had been unable to reform the courts through legislative means, yeomen began holding demonstrations at courthouses. Forming large groups, they surrounded the debtor courts and protested. By preventing anyone from entering the building, they stopped the courts from holding sessions and stopped more debt cases from being heard. Because they felt they were paying more than their share of taxes, and had been unable to obtain tax relief through the legislature, yeomen harassed tax collectors and other government officials.

To retaliate, the government of Massachusetts put out warrants for the arrests of the Regulator leaders. Vigilantes known as lighthorsemen rode into the countryside from Boston to harass yeomen and capture the ringleaders of the Regulator protests and uprisings. Several violent conflicts took place between Regulators and lighthorsemen. Some of the most active Regulators were captured by lighthorsemen and jailed. People began to fear the lighthorsemen, who rode through the night and woke people up, looking for suspected rebels. Believing that the state was tyrannical, and that, like England, it must be overthrown, the Regulators decided to take action. In order to arm themselves, they planned an attack on the Springfield arsenal.

Showdown at the Springfield Arsenal

On January 21, 1787, one thousand Regulators from Worcester and Middlesex counties marched to the town of Palmer, Massachusetts, east of the Springfield arsenal. That same day, three hundred Regulators from the western county of Berkshire marched for sixty miles in the snow to the Chicopee Bridge, just north of the arsenal. Also marching that day was a regiment of one thousand Hampshire County Regulators bound for the town of West Springfield.

Along their way, they placed guards at strategic points, such as the Boston Post Road and the Connecticut River ferry. Many of the Regulators were veterans of the Revolutionary War or the French and Indian War, a colonial conflict between England and France in which many American Indians participated. Some of the Regulators wore their old army uniforms. All of them placed sprigs of pine or some other evergreen in their caps, as they had when they fought with the Continental Army, to symbolize their resistance. The pine tree had long been a symbol of liberty in Massachusetts and had been printed on coins and flags. Now, as these Massachusetts farmers armed themselves for the cause of liberty, they once again stuck evergreen in their caps.

On the march to Springfield, some of the Regulators harassed shopkeepers who had taken farmers to court over small debts. On January 23, the rebels took several shopkeepers prisoner. They demanded that one store owner give their army supplies of beef, pork, and grain. Regulators targeted this store owner because he had taken dozens of farmers to court over debts owed to him.

By January 25, all of the Regulator regiments were in Springfield, ready for the three-pronged attack that had been planned by the captains of the different Regulator regiments. That afternoon, the regiments were to close in on the arsenal from their present positions just east, north, and west of the city.

Standing in their way were one thousand state militiamen headed by General William Shepard, who had been appointed by Massachusetts Governor James Bowdoin. Shepard's orders were to defend the arsenal from attack, but he had only one thousand men compared with the Regulators' two thousand. Nervous about being outnumbered, Shepard had requested reinforcements. Governor Bowdoin had granted his request. Another general, Benjamin Lincoln, with about three thousand men, had been sent from Boston. But General Lincoln and his men were marching westward through deep snow, and they were still two days away from Springfield. Meanwhile, Shepard was outnumbered and nearly surrounded by the rebels.

On January 25, the day the Regulators had planned to strike, one of the Regulator regiments from Hampshire County issued a final plea for peace. Luke Day, the captain of the regiment, wrote a letter to General Shepard, demanding that his troops surrender within twenty-four hours. Otherwise, the Regulators would launch their attack. Day then wrote to the other rebel regiments, telling them of the letter to Shepard and asking them not to attack until twenty-four hours had passed. But Day's letters were intercepted by some of General Shepard's men. His message never reached the other Regulators. General Shepard knew that even without Lincoln's reinforcements, he was now in a good position to put down the Regulators. Their force would be divided. Unaware that Day's regiment had

Benjamin Lincoln, a prominent general during the American Revolution, was sent to help put down the Regulator uprising.

stalled, the other Regulators to the north and east of Springfield marched as planned.

Around 4:00 P.M. on the afternoon of January 25, 1787, approximately thirteen hundred men approached the arsenal at Springfield. They must have wondered where the other one thousand Regulators were, but they did not retreat. Marching in half a foot of snow, the rebels approached the arsenal in two columns. They held their muskets to their shoulders. With less than one hundred fifty yards between them and the arsenal, the rebels halted. Seizing the opportunity, two of General Shepard's men rode up to the rebels on horseback with a message from the general. If they continued to advance, the message warned, they would be fired upon. Hoping it might deter them, General Shepard also wanted the men to know that inside the arsenal, among the militia, were men who had served in some of the same units as the Regulators during the Revolution. Some of them had been commanding officers. Under these officers, just a few years earlier, the Regulators had fought for the freedom of their country. Now, they had taken up arms against their countrymen. If they decided to attack the arsenal, they would be attacking the same men who had been their superior officers during the Revolutionary War.

Hearing this, one of the leading Regulators, Captain Adam Wheeler, a veteran, cried out, "That is all we want, by God!"[2] Daniel Shays brushed off the warning from the general's messengers. After holding a quick conference with his men, perhaps to discuss

THE
HISTORY
OF THE
INSURRECTIONS,
IN
MASSACHUSETTS,
In the YEAR MDCCLXXXVI,
AND THE
REBELLION
CONSEQUENT THEREON.

BY **GEORGE RICHARDS MINOT**, A. M.

PRINTED AT *WORCESTER,* MASSACHUSETTS,
BY **ISAIAH THOMAS.** MDCCLXXXVIII.

Historian George Richards Minot wrote the first history of Shays' Rebellion, published in 1788.

whether or not they should proceed without Luke Day's regiment, the soldiers resumed their fighting stance. Shays led them into battle, hollering, "March!"[3]

Inside the arsenal, General Shepard gave the order for his men to fire the cannons, but told the men to aim well over the heads of the rebels. He hoped the firing might stop the Regulators without actually causing any injury. The cannons blasted smoke and shot into the air, but the rebels continued to march. General Shepard ordered his men to fire over their heads once more. Again, the cannons were loaded with shot, packed, and fired. Undaunted, the rebels still marched. Now General Shepard ordered his men to fire the cannons directly into the center of the approaching ranks. Militiamen fired fourteen times. Four rebels in the center of the first row of Regulators were hit by cannon shot and killed. They lay dead, bleeding in the snow. Twenty other Regulators were wounded by cannon shot. In the smoke and confusion that followed, those who could still run retreated. The Regulators scattered, leaving the scene of violence and regrouping outside the city.

What could have caused these yeomen, just a few years after the revolution that had united Americans in a common patriotic cause, to take arms against their countrymen and their former commanding officers? Why had they deemed it necessary to spill blood in defense of their views? And what would happen to them now that their plan had failed?

2

LIFE AFTER THE REVOLUTION

The answer to why the Regulators attacked their fellow countrymen in the winter of 1787 may be found by investigating how life had changed in Massachusetts since the American Revolution. In many ways, life was more difficult than it had been before the war. After a long and costly war, the Americans had managed to defeat the British at the Battle of Yorktown in 1781. The Treaty of Paris, signed in 1783, officially ended hostilities with Great Britain. The United States became an independent nation, guided by a document known as the Articles of Confederation, which had been drafted by the Continental Congress in 1777. Adopted in 1781, the Articles of Confederation created a loose alliance of states, each governed by its own constitution. In 1780, when Massachusetts adopted its state constitution, citizens viewed it as the fulfillment of the goals of the revolution. Finally, they were self-governing.

Victory, however, had come at a price. The war had been an expensive undertaking, and the whole country faced serious war debt. Massachusetts' own share of

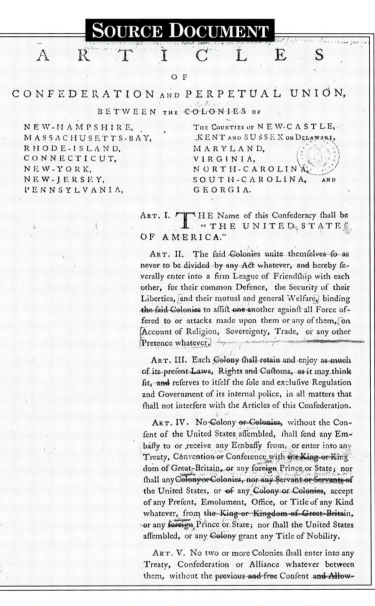

ARTICLES

OF

CONFEDERATION AND PERPETUAL UNION,

BETWEEN THE COLONIES OF

NEW-HAMPSHIRE,
MASSACHUSETTS-BAY,
RHODE-ISLAND,
CONNECTICUT,
NEW-YORK,
NEW-JERSEY,
PENNSYLVANIA,

THE COUNTIES OF NEW-CASTLE,
KENT AND SUSSEX ON DELAWARE,
MARYLAND,
VIRGINIA,
NORTH-CAROLINA,
SOUTH-CAROLINA, AND
GEORGIA.

ART. I. THE Name of this Confederacy shall be "THE UNITED STATES OF AMERICA."

ART. II. The said Colonies unite themselves so as never to be divided by any Act whatever, and hereby severally enter into a firm League of Friendship with each other, for their common Defence, the Security of their Liberties, and their mutual and general Welfare, binding the said Colonies to assist one another against all Force offered to or attacks made upon them or any of them, on Account of Religion, Sovereignty, Trade, or any other Pretence whatever.

ART. III. Each Colony shall retain and enjoy as much of its present Laws, Rights and Customs, as it may think fit, and reserves to itself the sole and exclusive Regulation and Government of its internal police, in all matters that shall not interfere with the Articles of this Confederation.

ART. IV. No Colony or Colonies, without the Consent of the United States assembled, shall send any Embassy to or receive any Embassy from, or enter into any Treaty, Convention or Conference with the King or Kingdom of Great-Britain, or any foreign Prince or State; nor shall any Colony or Colonies, nor any Servant or Servants of the United States, or of any Colony or Colonies, accept of any Present, Emolument, Office, or Title of any Kind whatever, from the King or Kingdom of Great-Britain, or any foreign Prince or State; nor shall the United States assembled, or any Colony grant any Title of Nobility.

ART. V. No two or more Colonies shall enter into any Treaty, Confederation or Alliance whatever between them, without the previous and free Consent and Allow-

The Articles of Confederation, a loose alliance agreement among the thirteen former British colonies, was the governing instrument of the United States in its early years.

the federal debt was more than one million pounds. In addition, Massachusetts had an internal debt of 1.3 million pounds, and it owed 250,000 pounds in back pay to soldiers and officers.[1] Unable to pay its Revolutionary War veterans, Massachusetts had issued the veterans paper notes. Known as continental securities, the state promised to redeem these notes in the future. However, because many veterans needed cash to pay their taxes and debts, they were forced to sell their notes to others for much less than they were worth. Since every town had supplied its own militia and supported it on credit during the war, individual towns had their own debts to pay, too. This all added up to a mountain of debt for Massachusetts, whose debt had never reached more than 100,000 pounds before the Revolutionary War.

Massachusetts was not the only state facing huge debt. Every state owed money. Delegates to the Continental Congress wanted to fix this disastrous financial situation. To raise money, they asked the states to agree to a change in the Articles of Confederation that would allow Congress to place a 5 percent tax on all imported goods. But not all the states wanted to give Congress the power to tax. Many feared that the national government would then become too powerful. However, without the power to tax, the national government could do little to lessen the financial problems of the states. The individual states, therefore, had to raise taxes to increase revenue.

Returning Home From the War

Some American soldiers who had survived the Revolutionary War returned to find their homes and land in disarray, their fields overgrown, and their families suffering from lack of food. Men had gone off to war and left their wives, daughters, mothers, and sisters to take their places in the fields and in their businesses. Women shouldered these burdens. They sent most of the crops they grew, the woolens they knitted, and the cloth they wove, to the men on the warfront. As a result, food shortages in some areas had affected the women, children, and old people, who had tried to keep the farms going while contributing much of what they produced to the war effort. Towns had passed high taxes to have enough money to supply soldiers with food and clothing. Townspeople had gone without basic provisions so that the army could be fed. Some generals paid their regiments' salaries out of their own pockets when there was no money from the state to pay them.

This was the climate of confusion and poverty to which soldiers returned home. They worked to rebuild their lives and property, but they were frustrated by a lack of cash and high taxes. The Continental, a paper bill printed by the Continental Congress, was no longer worth its face value. Paper currency printed by the state of Massachusetts was also devalued. During the war, rather than raising taxes even higher, most states had just printed more paper money to get necessary cash. Eventually, this overabundance of paper money caused inflation problems. In 1780, it took forty paper dollars to purchase one silver dollar.[2] "Not worth a Continental," a phrase referring to the devaluation of paper currency, became a popular saying of the day.[3]

Many soldiers came home from the revolution to find debts that had gone unpaid while they were away. Creditors harassed debtors to make them pay, but since paper currency had decreased in value, it took more of it to pay a debt. Meanwhile, gold and silver, or specie, was scarce.

Farmers wanted the government to issue paper money that would be honored at face value, and they wanted to clear up the confusion caused by the many different types of paper money in circulation. Merchants, however, opposed the use of paper money. Many of them, including Governor James Bowdoin, who was a merchant speculator, had bought up continental securities from veterans, paying only a fraction of their price. They hoped the state would eventually pay these notes at face value in specie, not in paper money, which depreciated quickly. They also did not want to see paper money continue to spread, because they did not want to have to accept devalued paper money in exchange for their goods. Merchants opposed the issuing of paper money because it would ruin them. Farmers, on the other hand, wanted paper money because they would be ruined without it. Thus merchants' opposition to paper currency and farmers' desire for it brought them into conflict.

Paper money issued by the state of Massachusetts (top) and the United States (bottom) in the 1780s were often worth far less than their face value. The saying "Not worth a Continental" became popular in the years after the American Revolution.

Lives of the Yeomen

Eighteenth-century farmers in central and western Massachusetts were primarily yeomen who grew only what they needed to make themselves comfortable. Often, they tilled just a portion of their land. Yeoman farmers grew a variety of crops sufficient to feed their families and animals and leave them with a small surplus. This surplus could then be traded with shopkeepers for manufactured items they could not produce themselves. In contrast, commercial farmers grew large quantities of marketable crops like hemp or flax (which were used to make rope and sailcloth) and then sold them for profit. Most farmers in New England, however, were yeomen. They outnumbered commercial farmers, making up 70 percent of the agrarian, or farming, population in rural New England.[4] Rural craftsmen were also considered yeomen. They performed their trade in exchange for food and other goods. Although they often owned small farms themselves, craftsmen such as shoemakers might trade the shoes they made to farmers in exchange for wheat or produce. They would also exchange their shoes with other people for services such as blacksmithing or medical care.

Paul Smith was a twenty-nine-year-old farmer in the Connecticut River valley town of Whately, Massachusetts, in 1784.[5] He had a wife and two children, and owned fifty-six acres of land. Yet Smith only cultivated fourteen acres, on which he grew enough food for his family and enough hay for his animals.

This also left him with a small surplus each year, which he exchanged for store-bought goods. Items such as nails or salt, which Smith could not make himself, he got by trading some of his surplus to the shopkeeper. In addition, Smith's wife spun wool into yarn, which the family could exchange for any other manufactured goods they needed, such as shoes, glass, forks, and knives. Smith, like other yeoman farmers, might have been able to cultivate more of his land, produce a larger surplus, and purchase even more manufactured goods. But clearing land and cultivating it was hard work for a single farmer, and was not considered necessary, so more often than not a farmer put only a portion of his land into productive use. This was their traditional method of farming.

Lives of the Merchants

On the coast of New England, as well as in inland market towns, merchants had a different way of life. Some of the wealthiest and largest merchant firms were located in commercial centers along the eastern seaboard such as Boston, Massachusetts, and Providence and Newport, Rhode Island. There were also many inland retailers and shopkeepers. In western Massachusetts, merchants tended to live in market towns such as Northampton, Amherst, Hadley, or Springfield. As members of commercial society, merchants had more personal wealth than most other citizens. The average value of the household furniture and goods in a Boston merchant's home, between 1725 and 1774, was 156 pounds. In contrast, the average value of household goods in a western Massachusetts farmer's home was only 26 pounds.[6]

Merchants and their families had more possessions, clothing, and luxury items than farm families did. They tended to live an affluent lifestyle, as shown by household inventories—records that list the items in a person's household and estate at the time of his or her death. Inventories were taken to insure that a person's will was executed properly, then they were filed and kept on record at courthouses. Because inventories often reveal the contents of people's homes, historians use them to investigate what life was like in the past. Household inventories show that by the end of the eighteenth century, people from the merchant class in Boston and other commercial centers were likely to own such luxury items as clocks, wigs, looking glasses, porcelain tea sets, books, and pictures. In contrast, yeoman farmers and craftsmen rarely owned any of these items.

Merchants spent their days in pursuit of the goods that could be bought at a low price and sold higher. Thomas Hancock, a wealthy Boston merchant, imported goods from England and then shipped these wares to shopkeepers all over New England. From the coast of Connecticut, up the Connecticut River, goods such as cotton imported from India and nails made in England found their way to buyers in western Massachusetts.[7] As a merchant, Hancock performed an important function by linking distant sellers to distant buyers. Hancock was careful to research what items consumers actually needed and wanted. Then he supplied country retailers with that kind of merchandise.

Stephen Hubbard was a shopkeeper in the western town of Northampton, Massachusetts, in the 1780s.[8] He stocked his shop with imported manufactured goods such as glass and iron, which he purchased from wholesalers in Boston and New York. Hubbard traded these goods to farmers in the Connecticut River valley in exchange for their agricultural surplus. Then Hubbard sent these crops down the Connecticut River to wholesalers in Hartford, who bought them and resold them in the West Indies, making a profit for themselves in the process. After the Revolutionary War, Great Britain barred American merchants from selling their goods in the British West Indies. The loss of this market made life more difficult for everyone, from wholesalers to retailers to farmers.

Conflict Between Yeomen and Merchants

Even a small inland merchant like Stephen Hubbard was wealthier than a yeoman farmer. Members of the merchant class were also better educated than the average yeoman. Because the merchant class enjoyed a more refined and modern lifestyle, many of its members looked down upon yeoman farmers as simple people.

"The manners of the town and country are so very different that I hardly know how to mention them together," argued an urban writer in the newspaper the *Massachusetts Centinel* in March 1784:

> The ideas of the country people are too often cribbed, narrow, and confined: all their notions are little; their minds want the expanding peculiar to the education of the great world; their desire for reading extends no farther than *Robinson Crusoe* or *Mr. John Bunyan's Pilgrim's Progress*; and their converse [is about] the regular diurnal [everyday] scandal of the neighborhood or village, for . . . there are no great and noble objects to amuse the mind.[9]

Yeoman farmers were similarly prejudiced against merchants. Yeomen thought merchants lacked virtue and honesty and did not know the value of hard work. "I believe this country would flourish faster if there were less white shirts and more black frocks," wrote one farmer to the *Hampshire Gazette* in 1786, referring to the white shirts worn by merchants and the black ones worn by farmers. "Let us oblige the merchants to shut up their shops and get their living by following the plough," he said, in the hopes that turning merchants into farmers would benefit the country.[10] As the American economy faltered after the Revolutionary War, merchants and yeomen began to distrust each other even more. The traditional agrarian way of life clashed with the developing commercial culture. Financial crisis soon brought them into conflict.

Financial Troubles

During and after the revolution, hard times had been brought on by war debt, inflation, and the losses sustained by the American shipping and fishing industries. Americans still traded with England, but after the war, under English commercial policy, they were not allowed to trade directly with the West Indies. This was England's way of punishing Americans for breaking away. The loss of the lucrative West Indies trade hurt Americans.

Immediately after the war, British merchants had sold American merchants goods on credit, but when American merchants were unable to pay their creditors, the British demanded repayment and refused to loan any more money. Many American merchants owed money to English creditors.

In order to make the money to pay them back, they needed to develop new markets for their goods. Now that the West Indies trade was gone, they had lost their major market. It was difficult for American merchants to sell imported goods at home, where money was scarce and people could not afford to buy unessential manufactured goods. American merchants had trouble selling their wares, but they still had to satisfy their creditors. To raise money to pay their British creditors, American merchants tried to collect all the money that was owed to them.

But times were hard for everyone, and many debtors were unable to pay their creditors. When merchants were unable to collect the money owed to them, they took legal action against debtors. As a result, the 1780s saw a dramatic increase in the number of debt suits. In rural Hampshire County in western

Massachusetts, there was a 263 percent increase in debt-related cases brought before the Court of Common Pleas from 1784 to 1786. Nearly three thousand cases were heard, most of them for small sums of less than twenty pounds.[11] An estimated one out of every four Massachusetts men had a debt suit brought against him between 1784 and 1786.[12] Other Massachusetts counties, including Worcester, Essex, Berkshire, and Bristol, also experienced sharp increases in the number of debt suits. Courts were clogged with cases against debtors. Citizens in other states had severe debt problems as well. Courthouses in Connecticut, New Hampshire, and Vermont were full of debtor cases.

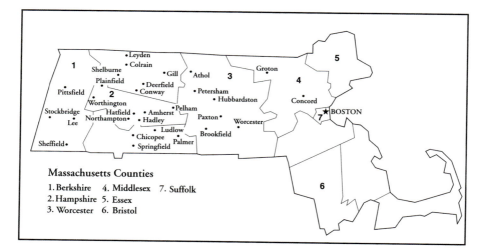

Massachusetts Counties
1. Berkshire   4. Middlesex   7. Suffolk
2. Hampshire   5. Essex
3. Worcester   6. Bristol

The towns and counties of western Massachusetts were the scene of many financial crises for farmers and other yeomen in the years after the American Revolution. County lines are as in present-day.

Many farmers owed money. Emerging market centers like Springfield, Worcester, and Northampton had involved local farmers in the market economy. Merchants would sell farmers imported manufactured goods, such as nails and cloth, on credit. Farmers would then raise surplus farm goods, which they would use to pay the shopkeepers back. They paid their debts when their crop was harvested. Using agricultural goods to pay debts was a common practice. However, during hard times, this barter system fell apart. Merchants had their own debts to pay, so they wanted to be paid in cash, not goods.

The Chain of Debt

When a merchant wholesaler (one who sells primarily to retailers, not the general public) became financially unstable, he demanded that the retailers with whom he did business pay back any money they owed him. Wholesalers often took retailers to court to get their money back. In order to pay the wholesaler, the retail shopkeepers were forced to take their own clients to court to collect any money that was owed to them. This created a chain reaction between creditors and debtors at all levels of the economy.

In the western market towns of Springfield, Northampton, Westfield, Deerfield, Hatfield, and Hadley, shopkeepers called in all the small debts owed to them by farmers, and they asked to be paid in cash. In order to pay their own creditors, the shopkeepers needed cash, not goods, since goods were difficult to resell in hard times. Most farmers owed only a few pounds, but they were accustomed to paying their debts seasonally with crops or labor. Most did not have cash. All they had was the surplus they grew. Farmers, therefore, were caught short when asked to pay their debts immediately in cash.

Yeomen who were unable to pay back their debts faced prosecution. Some had their land and goods taken from them by the courts. If a farmer was unable to pay his debt, his creditor could hire a lawyer and bring suit against him. If the court approved, the creditor could then seize and sell the debtor's property in order to collect his loan. A man who had owed a few pounds to a shopkeeper might have his property seized to pay back that sum, as well as what he owed in court and lawyer fees. In the early American legal system, the debtor had to pay court costs and lawyer's fees, so being taken to debtor's court was an expensive experience. Some farmers lost their cattle, sheep, and even their land.

Property was not always judged at fair value, either, as citizens of Greenwich, Massachusetts, complained to the state legislature in January 1786: "The constables are daily venduing [selling at public auction] our property both real and personal, our land after it is appraised by the best judges under oath is sold for about one-third of the value of it, our cattle about one-half the value."[13] Debtors came to hate lawyers, who profited at the expense of the poor. The seizure of their land was a horrifying prospect to yeoman farmers, for whom ownership of land was their only means of earning a living. Their land was one of the things for which they had fought during the revolution. As yeoman farmers in Conway, Massachusetts, explained, the

> *mortgage of our farms*—we cannot think of, with any degree of complacency. To be *tenants* to *landlords*, we know not who, and pay rents for lands, *purchased with our money*, and converted from howling *wilderness*, into fruitful fields, by the *sweat of our brow*, seems to carry with it in its nature truly shocking [consequences].[14]

Debtors lived in fear that their land and livelihoods might be taken from them by lawyers. They also feared another fate: being thrown into debtor's prison. Debtor's prison was a place where debtors were kept until someone paid their debt for them. Debtors were often housed in the same jail with thieves and murderers.

Life in Debtor's Prison

Debtor's prisons were overcrowded and unclean places. Cells were damp and often lacked proper light or ventilation. These conditions bred sickness and all kinds of problems. Some towns had separate debtor's jails and jails for other kinds of criminals, whereas others combined the two. One Massachusetts debtor's jail housed nearly ninety men for six months in a space that measured just 28 by 36 feet.[15] Conditions in debtor's prisons were so bad at the end of the eighteenth century that Worcester newspaper printer and editor Isaiah Thomas took up the cause of prison reform and sought to publicize the terrible jail conditions in

Massachusetts. In his crusade, Thomas used the case of Timothy Bigelow to advance his cause. Bigelow was a Revolutionary War veteran who became indebted after the war as he struggled to work his farm. Unable to pay his creditors, Bigelow was thrown into debtor's prison at the Worcester County jail. No one paid his debt for him, and Bigelow stayed in jail, where he became ill and eventually died in a dank cell.

Conditions in debtor's prisons were equally terrible in other Massachusetts counties. Samuel Ely, a former minister who later joined the Regulator movement, found himself in the Bristol County, Massachusetts, jail in March 1783 after failing to pay a debt. According to Ely's account of the time he spent in the jail, debtors had good reason to fear going to debtor's prison. Ely survived his time in debtor's prison "alive and that is all as I am full of boils and putrified [*sic*] sores all over my body and they make me stink alive, besides having some of my feet froze which makes it difficult to walk."[16]

A man sitting in debtor's prison could not earn any money to pay his way out. But creditors often insisted that someone who owed them money remain in jail, in the hopes that his friends or family would pay his debt in order to have him released. Sometimes this ploy worked. Other times, people remained in debtor's prison for their entire term with no way to pay their debt. The majority of people in debtor's prison were yeoman farmers, rural laborers, and craftsmen. Retailers and merchants were far less likely to serve time in debtor's prison, because they were usually able to find the resources to pay their debt.

Higher Taxes

In addition to the chain of debt linking wholesalers, retailers, and farmers, taxation created another burden for Massachusetts citizens, especially farmers. Taxes had been increasing in Massachusetts since 1776, and after the revolution they increased dramatically as Massachusetts tried to pay off its war debt. Though all the New England states levied higher taxes after the war, Massachusetts had the most unbearable policy. The state asked for nearly one third of each person's income in taxes. Worse, these taxes now had to be paid in gold and silver, not paper money or goods.

This was an especially terrible blow to yeomen, who, whenever possible, preferred to pay their taxes with labor rather than with cash. Previously, in places like Springfield, Massachusetts, as much as 90 percent of the inhabitants worked out their highway taxes by fixing and improving the roads, rather than paying in cash.[17]

People now had to come up with gold or silver, not paper money or goods, to pay their taxes. Yet many taxpayers were veterans of the Revolutionary War, and they themselves had not been paid fully for their service. Compounding the problem for farmers was a new tax policy that placed higher taxes on land than it did on individual income. Farmers, who owned land but had little money, found the new property taxes hard to shoulder. Adding to the tax burden, in 1781

Massachusetts introduced an excise, or internal tax, on items such as alcohol, tea, and horse carriages and coaches that were made, sold, or used within the state. The western towns complained that this tax was rigged against them in favor of eastern dwellers. For example, they complained, the excise on homemade alcohol like hard cider, which was frequently made by farmers, was twice that of the tax on rum, the alcohol commonly sold by New England merchants. All this added up to an intolerable burden for yeoman farmers. In the 1780s, the General Court, as the state legislature was called, was flooded with petitions from Massachusetts towns, asking for relief from such high taxes.

Yeomen Seek to Ease the Tax Burden

Hoping for relief, yeomen contacted their state representatives and demanded that paper money be accepted at face value. They hoped to be able to use the paper money they had been stuck with, money no one wanted to accept. When this initiative failed, the yeomen asked the legislature to suspend all debtor cases until economic times improved. Hoping to buy time to come up with the money they owed, yeomen wanted the courts to halt proceedings against debtors until the debtors were better able to repay their creditors. But this bill failed to pass through the legislature in Boston.

Proposals for debtor relief came primarily from farmers in the western part of the state, which was much more depressed economically. By 1783, sixty-four towns in the western counties of Hampshire and Berkshire had not paid their taxes fully.[18] By comparison, only twenty towns in the eastern Massachusetts counties of Middlesex and Essex were delinquent.[19] This was because the western counties were overwhelmingly populated by small-scale yeoman farmers who found the tax burden difficult to bear. In parts of Berkshire County, Massachusetts, along the western border with New York, people still lived in frontier conditions. The residents, trying to establish farms in these remote, unsettled, and untilled areas, found the higher taxes especially difficult to pay.

When yeoman farmers were unsuccessful in passing paper money laws or suspending legal actions against debtors, they tried to pass a "tender law." The tender law would allow them to repay creditors with crops or goods. During the Revolutionary War, Massachusetts had passed a tender law, which, for a limited amount of time, had made it possible for debts to be paid with personal property, such as cattle. This law, passed while America was short on cash and specie due to the war, was designed to make it possible for debtors to pay off their debts with personal goods. As the postwar economic recession set in, many people began asking for the return of the tender law. Yeomen wanted to be able to pay their taxes and their debts in goods. Many felt that a new tender law might be the only way for them to make good on their debts and taxes while times remained hard. "Unless debtors are permitted to pay their private debts with property, both real and personal," argued farmers in Dracut, Massachusetts, it would be "out of the power of a great part of the community, as well as the inhabitants of this town, to extricate themselves from the labyrinth of debt."[20]

Merchants, however, were opposed to a tender law. They did not want to have to accept goods instead of cash. With the loss of the West Indies trade, they had no market for the goods and agricultural surpluses with which they would be paid, and thus no way to turn a profit on this kind of payment. They needed cash, not goods, to pay their own debts.

Massachusetts yeomen had believed that their lives would improve after the revolution, which they had fought at the expense of their lives. Now that the war had been won, they were worse off than ever before, facing debt, high taxes, and the potential loss of their land. Determined to find solutions to their problems, they continued to lobby for legislation that would improve their situation.

PETITIONS AND PROTEST

Battered by postwar economic troubles, in debt, and watching their friends and neighbors lose their personal property to creditors, yeoman farmers were determined to find solutions to their problems. From 1781 to 1785, yeomen in Massachusetts wrote letters to the newspapers, publicly explaining their grievances. They also petitioned the legislature and held conventions to discuss their problems. They tried to find relief for the debt and taxes that plagued them. Yeomen blamed their situation on the high taxes that had been levied after the American Revolution to pay for the cost of war, and the lack of money since 1780 that had resulted from the devaluation of paper money and the scarcity of gold and silver. The yeomen looked to three reforms that they thought would bring them a better life: a new paper currency, lower taxes, and reform of the debtor courts. To promote these reforms, yeomen held conventions in many towns and counties. Delegates from all over Massachusetts joined in the discussion at these conventions.

Holding Conventions

According to the Massachusetts state constitution, which was adopted in 1780, the people had the right of assembly and petition. Establishing this right was important to the people of Massachusetts, who had been denied the right of assembly by the British in the years leading up to the Revolutionary War. To organize resistance to British policies, they had been forced to meet secretly. Now that Massachusetts had a constitution of its own, it granted its citizens the right to assemble as they pleased.

Exercising this right, on February 11, 1782, a group of yeomen convened in Hadley, Massachusetts, to discuss the state's tax policies and the record numbers of debt suits that had flooded the courts. The prevailing belief at this convention was that debt-related suits in the courts needed to be suspended until taxes were reduced or economic times improved. Though yeomen had tried unsuccessfully to pass this measure in the legislature once before, they continued to promote it as the best means of surviving financial hardship.

The Hadley convention inspired other people to unite to discuss common concerns. In 1782, yeomen also held conventions in Worcester, Pittsfield, and Hatfield. Individual towns elected delegates to represent their voters at these conventions. Delegates discussed their desire for a tender law and the need for a suspension of debt cases. Everyone wanted relief from high taxes and yeomen complained that the tax structure favored mercantile interests and worked against landed interests. Many delegates expressed concern that the government only served the interests of commercial men.

Mistrust of Government

Yeomen had long worried that the Massachusetts government was dominated by mercantile, or commercial, interests. They felt that their interests were not always promoted by the legislature. At conventions held all over the state in 1782, delegates expressed concern with the way state officials handled money. They also demanded better accountability and wanted to know how their tax dollars were being spent. They asked the legislature to send them an annual report of expenditures. They also argued that government salaries, particularly the governor's salary of eleven hundred pounds a year, were too high and should be reduced. Many farmers blamed high taxes on the high cost of maintaining the courts and paying the salaries of judges and other government officials. They did not necessarily trust the government to run itself efficiently.

In part, yeomen blamed their lack of representation on the fact that the legislature met in Boston. Given the great distance that representatives from the western towns had to travel, it was expensive and difficult for these western Massachusetts representatives to attend the legislature sessions regularly. In contrast, it was geographically easier and much less expensive for eastern representatives to attend every session in Boston. This fact made it easier for mercantile interests to

The old statehouse in Boston, where the legislature met, as it looked in Daniel Shays' time.

obtain a majority vote over the interests of the country towns. As a result, many westerners wanted the legislature to meet in a country location, where it would not be dominated by commercial interests.

Demanding Judicial Reform

Perhaps unfairly, yeomen blamed the explosion of debt cases in the courts on lawyers, who profited by prosecuting the ever-growing number of debtors from the western counties. Lawyers were so hated in country areas that they became the butt of many jokes. One popular joke of the day told of two lawyers who met a wagon on the road. The lawyers asked the wagon driver, "Why is your fore-horse [front horse] so fat and the others so lean?" The wagon driver, knowing the men were lawyers, responded: "My fore-horse is a lawyer, and the others are his clients."[1]

In eighteenth-century Massachusetts, debtors had to pay the court costs and lawyers' fees when a creditor brought them to court. Yeomen felt lawyers charged too much, and they demanded a reduction in the fees. Being taken to court was expensive. To avoid the high cost, yeomen argued that a justice of the peace, as opposed to the formal Court of Common Pleas, ought to be able to rule on all debt cases. Under the law, justices of the peace were only allowed to preside over very small debt cases involving less than forty shillings. Farmers wanted this amount raised because it was much less costly for a debtor to go before one justice of the peace than a full court. It was also much easier for a debtor to find a justice of the peace in his own community than it was to travel to the county courthouse. If justices of the peace were allowed to handle more cases, the yeomen argued, there would be no need for a Court of Common Pleas. Many yeomen wanted to do away with the courts altogether, arguing that it was expensive for the state to maintain the judicial bodies. They felt that many court functions, including the registering of deeds, could be better handled by town clerks or justices of the peace.

Convention delegates wrote petitions containing lists of their grievances along with their suggestions for judicial reform and debtor relief. Then they sent copies of their petitions to the state legislature. Whether held at Hadley, Hatfield, Worcester, or Pittsfield, all the conventions concluded that country voices needed to be heard in Boston and that something must be done to remedy the desperate straits into which so many yeomen had fallen due to debt and hard times.

The effect of these conventions was to organize protesters and unite them in a common cause. The conventions also spread the news of the ways in which farmers had suffered and increased public awareness about what could be done to remedy these grievances. Not everyone approved of conventions, however. Some merchants and lawyers maintained that they were unlawful and had no place in a republican form of government. Letters to the editor in Massachusetts newspapers accused the farmers of being "treasonable to the state" and attempting to undermine the government by holding conventions.[2] But this was not the case. The majority of people represented at the conventions did not want to overthrow the government. Still, some of them felt it might be necessary to interfere with the workings of government temporarily in order to achieve their goals.

From Petitions to Action

When they received no response from their petitions to the legislature, some yeomen decided to take stronger action. On February 26, 1782, a mob of three hundred yeomen from Berkshire County tried to obstruct the proceedings of the Court of Common Pleas in Pittsfield. The Court of Common Pleas was responsible for hearing debtor cases. The yeomen believed that if they prevented the court from conducting business, they could prevent suits against debtors from being heard. Since they had been unsuccessful in getting the legislature to suspend debt cases in the courts, they were now attempting to accomplish this suspension themselves.

In April 1782, the outspoken Samuel Ely instigated an attack on the Hampshire County debtor court in Northampton. Ely was a Yale graduate who had long advocated that yeomen should rise up against the shopkeepers who pressed them for the small sums they owed. Ely and a group of yeomen attempted to stop the Northampton court from meeting, but the town militia halted them in front of the courthouse. Ely was arrested on the scene, but a few months later a group of farmers led by Reuben Dickinson, who later became a prominent figure in Shays' Rebellion, tried to rescue Ely from prison. Ely managed to escape, but three more yeomen were arrested in the process. Protesting these new arrests, five hundred farmers demonstrated in front of the Northampton jail. They demanded the release of the prisoners. Intimidated by the angry mob, jail officials released the men.

Inspired by the success of the Ely incident, yeomen across the state began to take action when they felt threatened. From 1782 onward, there was an increase in the number of disturbances involving yeoman protesters and the state. In September 1782, a mob of yeomen in Berkshire County rescued a pair of oxen that were being taken from their owner as payment for a debt. Trying to maintain order, the county sheriff raised his own mob of pro-government men to counter the yeomen, and they arrested twenty-one yeomen in connection with the incident.

In 1783, tax collectors were attacked by angry yeomen as they passed through Worcester County. Job Shattuck, another prominent figure in Shays' Rebellion, enlisted men to help him beat up tax collectors. Hampshire County yeomen gathered in May 1783 to prevent the debtor court from meeting at Springfield. The men positioned themselves at the entrances to the court and stopped people from entering. A pro-government mob showed up to oppose them. Eventually, the yeomen left, but not before some of them were hauled off to jail.

Discontent continued to grow among the farmers of western and central Massachusetts, but not everyone believed in violent forms of protest. Many advocated peaceful reform. In 1783, peaceful conventions were held in Hatfield, Hadley, and Deerfield. This time, they seemed to have an impact on the legislature. In 1784, the legislature passed two acts to provide relief for debtors. The first allowed a debtor whose land was seized to recover that land if he paid his debt, and the interest on it, within one year. In addition, any personal property seized by a creditor could not be auctioned for four days. This allowed the debtor a little more time to raise the money he owed. The second act passed by the legislature addressed a long-standing concern among the yeomen. This act made it possible for a justice of the peace to handle debtor suits involving up to four pounds. While it did not do away with the debtor courts completely, it was a small improvement.

The passage of these two small debtor relief acts was welcomed, but it was not enough to appease farmers in the western and central parts of the state. Yeomen continued to petition the legislature for laws that would make it easier for them to pay their taxes and their debts. But the state legislature ended its session in July 1786 without addressing these concerns or responding to the many lists of grievances it had received from various yeoman conventions. Farmers complained that their demands for a new paper money had not yet been met. A new tender law, which would have made it possible for people to pay debts and taxes with agricultural goods, had not been enacted. Yeomen could still have their property seized to pay their debts. The legislature had not suspended debtor courts or reduced lawyers' fees.

Grievances of the Yeomen

Yeomen responded to the legislature's inaction on their behalf by holding more conventions. Delegates from fifty towns in Hampshire County attended a three-day convention in Hatfield in August 1786. All of the delegates had been elected by voters in their towns, and many of them were the leading men of their towns. The Hatfield convention produced a list of grievances and resolves that was published. The delegates outlined the position of western yeomen on a number of key points. The list of grievances they created represented the bulk of complaints lodged by yeomen against the government, and also contained some guidelines for what they felt should be done:

1. Yeomen did not see the need for two organized bodies in the legislature. Under the Massachusetts state constitution, the state legislature consisted of both a House of Representatives and a Senate. The requirements for becoming a senator were stricter than those for representatives. Senators were required to hold more property or have personal estates valued at 600 pounds or more. Yeoman farmers expressed the concern that members of the Senate were not as responsive to the public as were members of the House of Representatives and suggested eliminating the Senate altogether.

2. Yeomen thought all government officials should be elected by the people annually, not appointed by the governor. In this way, they hoped to throw out officials who were not responsive to the public.

3. Yeomen did not see the need for an elaborate court system. They wanted to downsize the courts.

4. Yeomen wanted court and lawyers' fees reduced.

5. Yeomen felt that the excise discriminated against them. They wanted it recomputed to be more equally distributed between merchants and yeomen.

6. Yeomen wanted government officials' salaries reduced.

7. Yeomen felt the present method of paying government securities (IOU notes) was unfair to

them. Soldiers had been issued government security notes as compensation for their military service, and many of them were forced to cash these notes in at less than face value after the war. Then, after the notes had been bought by merchants at a discounted rate, the government had changed its policy and offered to pay the notes in specie at full value, benefiting the merchants. Plus, the money to finally pay the notes in full had come from high taxes that had been levied on the populace, especially yeomen.

8. Yeomen wanted more time to pay their taxes, and to be able to use goods and services as payment.

9. Yeomen felt that taxes were unequally levied between landed and commercial interests. They wanted to fix this problem.

10. Yeomen objected to the legislature's meeting in Boston. They felt it should meet more centrally, and that it should be removed from the sphere of influence of commercial interests in Boston.

11. Yeomen were upset that the legislature, which they had asked to send them an annual list of appropriations and expenses, had not yet done so.

12. Yeomen wanted their representatives to pass laws to issue paper money that would be legal tender and equivalent to hard currency.

13. Yeomen wanted the legislature to meet immediately to address their grievances.

14. Finally, yeomen at the Hatfield convention asked that people avoid unlawful assembly such as joining mobs until a constitutional method of resolving their problems had been obtained.

At the same time that the Hatfield convention was meeting to discuss the ways in which the yeomen of western and central Massachusetts felt disconnected from the state, people in Maine, which at that time was part of the state of Massachusetts, were beginning to agitate for separation. Massachusetts yeomen wanted the capital moved to a country town where they could receive greater representation, and citizens in Maine felt the same way. They argued that Boston was too far from Maine and that it was impossible for them to receive adequate representation from such a distance.

Separatists in Maine held conventions to discuss seceding from (leaving) Massachusetts. Maine's separatist stirrings annoyed Massachusetts officials, and it did not make them any more responsive to the dissension that was occurring in western and central Massachusetts. Perhaps they were reluctant to make any concessions to Massachusetts yeomen for fear that Maine would demand similar treatment.

Regulator Activity in Other States

Massachusetts men were not the first farmers to rise up against their government, or to complain that commercial interests were using the government for their own purposes. In the late 1760s and early 1770s, a group of Scotch-Irish frontiersmen and farmers, calling themselves Regulators, rose up against the government in North and South Carolina. They protested the fact that the Carolina governments were controlled by wealthy planters who lived on the eastern seaboard and seemed unconcerned with activities in the western part of the colonies. In South Carolina, the Regulators complained that there was little law enforcement in the western part of the province, and what little there was seemed to be rigged against them. So they formed their own vigilante mobs of Regulators, who patrolled and policed the region. The North Carolina Regulators, protesting what they felt was an unfair tax burden, finally came to blows with eastern militias and lost at the Battle of Alamance in 1771.

Carolina Regulators may have taken their name from the fact that they planned to regulate, or police, the countryside. The name may also have come from the fact that they acted like a militia, and their movements resembled the regular movements of an army. Given the parallels between the Regulators in the Carolinas and yeomen in Massachusetts, it is not surprising that Massachusetts farmers chose to use the name Regulators for themselves and their cause.

Events in other states during the 1780s show that Massachusetts farmers were not alone in their dissatisfaction with government. The tax policies of the United States government under the Articles of Confederation had angered farmers everywhere who feared that government was not acting in their best interests. When they were unable to find recourse through the legislature, these men resorted to defying the law.

For example, when New Hampshire was framing its constitution, its western towns became upset when the legislature refused to grant equal representation to all towns. As a result, western New Hampshire towns refused to acknowledge the constitutional government that was established. Instead, they insisted that the Declaration of Independence, issued in 1776, had made the people free to act on their own. They claimed that they had made no contract with the constitution and that legal power thus remained in the hands of the people. Like the Regulators in Massachusetts, New Hampshire yeomen used the rhetoric of revolution they had learned while opposing Great Britain.

In September 1786, a group of farmers-turned-rebels descended on the state house in Exeter, New Hampshire, obstructing official business and demanding paper money reforms. The farmers were desperate for paper currency, because they had no specie and needed some way to pay their taxes and debts. New Hampshire had no sympathy for these protesters. It sent armed pro-government citizens, called lighthorsemen, after the rebels and captured many of them. The captured rebels were then publicly humiliated or imprisoned.

Other states followed equally harsh policies against insurgents. In Connecticut, yeoman rebels had planned to obstruct the New Haven debtor court in the fall of 1786, but they were apprehended by state officials, and arrested. That same fall, Vermont yeomen attempted to disrupt debtor courts, but they were quickly put down by state militiamen. Unlike

Members of the Regulator movement sometimes turned to violence to express their feelings about the money situation in Massachusetts. Here, a member of the movement attacks a tax collector.

Massachusetts, other states took immediate action to forcibly put down any uprisings.

Blaming the Trouble on the British

People who opposed the Regulators, including many merchants and lawyers, blamed the discontent on the British. They feared that their old enemy was at work and that it was Tories (Americans who had remained loyal to England during the revolution) and the British who were stirring up this resentment against the Massachusetts government. They blamed British sympathizers for somehow creating this resistance and organizing conventions in order to undermine the state. Some Massachusetts citizens even believed the British were sending riders throughout the counties to stir up resistance. They worried that the British government had promised to support the rebellious farmers.

Despite this paranoia about British involvement in yeoman discontent, there is no evidence that the British were involved in yeoman uprisings. None of the yeomen who became Regulators had been Tories. Despite what some government officials thought, not all yeoman farmers advocated the overthrow of the government. Nor were they allying with the British against the United States. Most yeomen wanted reform, and if it meant closing courts temporarily, they were willing to do it. Only later, when they felt they had no choice left, did some of the Regulators take up arms against their government.

Obstructing the Courts

Delegates to the Hatfield convention in 1786 had called for peace and condemned mob action. However, just a few days after the convention ended, fifteen hundred armed men assembled in Northampton and tried to prevent the courts from holding session. The three leaders of this movement—Captain Luke Day of West Springfield, Captain Joseph Hinds of Greenwich, and Lieutenant Joel Billings of Amherst—appointed a committee of men to tell the judges that they did not want the court to conduct any official business until their grievances had been remedied. Under pressure, the judges agreed to halt their work at the courthouse, and the mob left.

After the incident at the Northampton courthouse, mob activity increased. Mobs prevented courts from operating in Hampshire, Berkshire, Bristol, Middlesex, and Worcester counties. Alarmed by this widespread obstruction of justice, the governor of Massachusetts, James Bowdoin, tried to get the local militias to put down these mobs. But too many of the western militiamen sided with the rebels. They refused to act against them. All across Massachusetts, militiamen deserted the militia rather than act against their countrymen. In fact, many militiamen deserted their posts to join the rapidly growing rebel movement, which was becoming a militia itself.

Who Were the Rebels?

The people who became involved in rebellious activity against Massachusetts in the 1780s were mainly yeoman farmers, craftsmen, and laborers from the central and western counties and the inland rural areas of Massachusetts. A few professional men, such as former debtor court judge William Whiting, joined the Regulators. But most of the rebels were farmers. Many were also debtors. All had suffered from high taxes and hard times. Quite a few were veterans, having served as officers and soldiers during the French and Indian or Revolutionary wars.

Adam Wheeler, who emerged as one of the leaders of the movement, was representative of many of the yeomen who became Regulators. A well-regarded citizen from Hubbardston, Captain Wheeler was a French and Indian War veteran and a Revolutionary War veteran who had

James Bowdoin was the governor of Massachusetts who faced the task of dealing with the Regulators.

fought at the Battle of Bunker Hill. To support the yeomen's cause, Captain Wheeler raised a company of one hundred Regulators from Hubbardston and marched with them to the Worcester courthouse, helping to obstruct the courts there in the fall of 1786.

The yeomen who became Regulators were primarily of Scotch-Irish or English descent, as were most New Englanders at that time. Similarly, the majority of Regulators, like most New Englanders, were Protestants. They belonged to the Congregational Church, the established church in Massachusetts at the time. Only a few African Americans joined the Regulators. This was because Regulators tended to live in inland rural areas. In the eighteenth century, most African Americans in New England lived in coastal towns and cities. Records show that there were at least three African-American yeomen—Aaron Carter of Colrain, Tobias Green of Plainfield, and Moses Sash of Worthington—all of whom lived in western Massachusetts, who joined the Regulators and participated in rebel activities.

Common Bonds Among the Regulators

Often, more than one man in a family would join the Regulators. On a list of sixty-nine Regulators from Pelham in 1787, more than half the surnames appeared more than once. Some surnames appeared as many as five times.[3] So many Regulators with the same last name in one town indicated that, typically, more than one person in a family was involved in the Regulator cause.

Along with common economic situations, kinship ties may have encouraged family members to join the movement together. Fathers and sons frequently participated in rebel activities together, drilling with their regiment or helping to obstruct the courts. Similarly, if a farmer was taken to debtor's court and lost his farm, his neighbors would be more likely to join the movement, if for no other reason than to make sure the same fate did not befall them. Community and family ties were an important organizing force among the Regulators.

Another factor that helped the Regulator movement was the flow of information from one Massachusetts county to another. Since the majority of eighteenth-century New Englanders could read, New England produced tens of thousands of newspapers and almanacs in the 1780s. Even small towns printed or received such publications, many of which were distributed weekly.[4] The publication and distribution of these periodicals provided a means of communication for rural areas like western and central Massachusetts. Though newspapers usually took a pro-government stance, they often printed letters to the editor that expressed the Regulators' point of view. Newspapers also carried news of court proceedings, and rebels could read the papers to find out when and where a court was going to be in session.

Taverns provided another means of communication. They had played a vital role in the organization of the American Revolution, and they continued to be one of the few places where people could gather to socialize, hear the latest news, and discuss their concerns. In Pelham, where Daniel Shays lived, the Conkey Tavern provided a comfortable place for men to meet, get information, and discuss their problems.

The Regulators Encounter Government Force

Through personal communication and newspapers, the Regulators knew that the Supreme Judicial Court, which met only a few times each year, had scheduled a session in Springfield for September 1786. The Regulators also knew that this court was supposed to decide the fate of the yeomen who had earlier obstructed the proceedings of the Northampton court. They were anxious to stop this court from meeting.

So in September 1786, a group of eleven hundred Regulators banded together in Springfield to obstruct the Supreme Judicial Court. Some of the Regulators had armed themselves with clubs. However, General William Shepard, commander of the Hampshire militia, had guessed that the Regulators might show up. To counter them, he had organized eight hundred men, arming them with weapons from the federal arsenal in Springfield. When the Regulators arrived, they found that Shepard and his men had already occupied the courthouse. However, the Regulators outnumbered

Shepard's men, and they were able to enter the building. When a small group of Regulators spoke to the Supreme Judicial Court judges, asking that they suspend all action, a standoff resulted. Regulators, with sprigs of evergreen jutting out of their caps, stared down Shepard's men, who had stuck slips of paper in their hats so they would not be identified as rebels. Though the judges refused to comply with the Regulators' demands, they were unable to hold court because not all the grand jury members were present. At the end of the day, each side claimed it had won a victory.

Daniel Shays

Chief among the Regulators at the Springfield courthouse that day was a thirty-nine-year-old farmer named Daniel Shays. Born in Hopkington, Massachusetts, in 1747, Shays had settled in Pelham, Massachusetts, with his wife, Abigail. Shays owned nearly one hundred acres, only three of which were under cultivation.

He had been living in Pelham at the time of the American Revolution. He had joined a company of minutemen (soldiers who responded quickly to the threat of a British attack) and responded to the Lexington alarm after colonists and British first fired on one another on April 19, 1775. The captain of his company was Reuben Dickinson of Amherst, who also later became a Regulator. Shays proved to be a good soldier. He was promoted for bravery at the Battle of Bunker Hill and eventually rose to the rank of captain.

Daniel Shays lived in this house in Pelham, Massachusetts.

Shays became a member of a fraternal order known as the Freemasons while serving in the Revolutionary War in New York, and he joined Masonic Lodge No. 2 at Albany in 1778. He was present at the surrender of British General John Burgoyne at Saratoga and at the storming of Stony Point. His bravery so impressed the Marquis de Lafayette, a French general who had joined the American fight against England, that the general later presented Shays with a ceremonial sword.

Shays left the military in 1780 and returned to Pelham. At some point, he fell into debt. He sold the sword Lafayette had given him to raise money. In 1784, Shays was taken to court over a twelve-pound debt. A few months later, a shopkeeper in Brookfield prosecuted Shays for a three-pound debt. Though he was a debtor, Shays was well respected in Pelham. He was known for the time he had served as a town warden and was frequently seen drilling the town militia in front of the Conkey Tavern in Pelham.

He was also one of the many yeomen who gathered at the Clapp Tavern in Amherst and at the Conkey Tavern to drink, socialize, and discuss political issues such as debt, taxation, and the lack of representation in the western counties. Shays represented the town of Pelham at several yeoman conventions. Eventually, like many other men from Pelham, he decided to join the

The Conkey Tavern, built in 1758, served as the site of many important incidents in Shays' Rebellion.

Regulator movement. But unlike other Regulators, Shays would soon have his name linked with the movement forever.

Shays helped lead the Regulators in their occupation of the Springfield courthouse in September 1786. And he was one of only a few Regulators who met with the judges there. His signature had also appeared on several documents written by the Regulators. Gradually, he came to be recognized by his fellow yeomen and by the government as one of the leaders of the Regulators, although Shays claimed that he had never sought a leadership role.

The Legislature Cracks Down on the Regulators

The day after the standoff between Regulators and state militiamen at the Springfield courthouse, the

SOURCE DOCUMENT

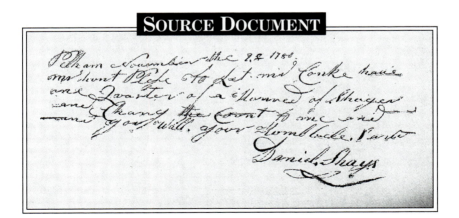

Daniel Shays' handwriting, which appeared on several documents in connection with the Regulator movement, is seen here.

Massachusetts legislature met in Boston. Amid reports that one third of the population of the state—and an even higher percentage in rural areas—supported the Regulator cause, the legislature responded to the incident at the Springfield courthouse by enacting repressive measures against the Regulators.

First, it suspended the writ of habeas corpus, the requirement that a law enforcement officer have evidence against a suspect in order to imprison him or her. Without habeas corpus, anyone the governor considered dangerous to the state could be arrested. These suspects could be imprisoned without bail. They could also be tried in any Massachusetts county, a move designed to prevent sympathetic local juries from letting them off easy.

Next, the legislature passed the Riot Act to prevent the Regulators from organizing. This law, designed by former revolutionary and patriot leader Samuel Adams, authorized sheriffs and justices of the peace to order an armed crowd to disperse. Adams used the same tactic against the Regulators that the British had used against him prior to the Revolutionary War. By preventing groups from meeting, the legislature hoped to prevent uprisings from occurring. Under the Riot Act, the failure of an armed crowd to disperse would result in arrest, imprisonment, and seizure of personal property. Mobs had been useful in resisting the British prior to the revolution, and people who were upset with the new government tried to use these same methods now. But even once-fervent patriots such as

Samuel Adams felt that the time for mob action had passed. Like many other revolutionaries, Adams had changed his mind about conventions and mobs after the revolution was over. He now argued that "popular Committees and County Conventions are not only useless but dangerous" to the progress and stability of the new nation.[5]

Hoping to suppress rebellion among the Regulators, the Massachusetts legislature also passed the Militia Act during its fall 1786 session. The Militia Act declared that "any officer or soldier who shall begin, excite, cause, or join in any mutiny or sedition" will be subject to "such punishment as by a court martial shall be inflicted."[6]

The Militia Act, together with the Riot Act and the suspension of the writ of habeas corpus, created a very inhospitable climate for protesters such as the Regulators. People suspected of being Regulators could now be arrested and detained without bail on the grounds that they put the safety of Massachusetts in danger. They could be held in jail without any evidence. Finally, to try to get the Regulators to surrender, the legislature also passed an Indemnity Act, which pardoned everyone who had helped obstruct the courts up to the time of the passage of the act if they would come forward and sign an oath of allegiance to the state before January 1, 1787.

After this battery of measures aimed at crushing rebellion, the legislature finally passed some legislation to assist debtors. Though the state had previously

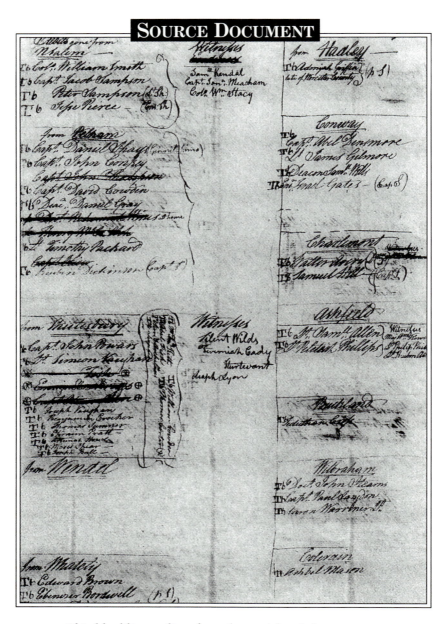

This blacklist, or list of people considered dangerous or suspicious, of Hampshire County Regulator leaders was compiled by Massachusetts Attorney General Robert Treat Paine.

demanded that taxes be paid in specie, it now allowed citizens to pay their taxes in goods—such as beef, grain, or butter—which could be brought to selected stores and exchanged as payment. A new tender law was passed, this time stipulating that creditors could not seize any tools or goods that were necessary to a person's trade. Creditors were also prevented from seizing household furniture or farm equipment. This version of the tender law also required that any goods seized by a creditor first had to be appraised by three different neutral parties, in order to ensure that the goods would be assessed at fair market value.

Despite these few favorable pieces of legislation, the actions of the legislature were not well received in western counties such as Berkshire and Hampshire, where there were large numbers of Regulators. The Riot and Militia acts and the legislature's suspension of habeas corpus aroused the wrath of yeomen who felt these measures were repressive and tyrannical.

The right to assemble had seemed essential to patriots in Massachusetts before the revolution, but with the passage of the Riot Act, yeomen felt that their right to assemble as they pleased was being infringed by the very people who had once insisted upon it. In the 1770s, Massachusetts patriots had formed mobs to close the courts, disrupt the government, and protest British policy in the hopes of finding some remedy for their grievances. "Did they give the opprobrious [disgraceful] epithet of mobs to the leaders of the measures in those days?" asked the citizens of Suffolk

County, Massachusetts, in 1784. "Do not the fears and jealousies of the good people of the State at this day spring from the *like source?*"[7]

Orderly conventions had been held in western Massachusetts for years. Only in the summer of 1786, when they grew larger, did these conventions begin to attract much public attention. That fall, the Riot and Militia acts attempted to prevent armed citizens from gathering or demonstrating against the government. Conventions were still legal, as long as the participants were not armed. But since the Regulators acted as a militia and carried arms, they would have to break the law if they wanted to continue to rally and obstruct the courts. The actions of the legislature had pushed the Regulators one step closer to armed rebellion.

The repressive acts passed by the Massachusetts legislature in the autumn of 1786 overshadowed the few debtor relief laws it did pass. For the Regulators, it was a case of too little, too late. The Regulator movement continued to gain momentum. Just a few weeks after the legislature ended its session in November 1786, the Regulators acted again. This time, they met in Worcester and prevented the courts from meeting there. Most of the Regulators who participated in the Worcester demonstration had not heard of the Indemnity Act. The Worcester militia was called to oppose the rebels who obstructed the courthouse, but many of the militiamen were sympathetic to the Regulators and refused to act. As a result, the Regulators succeeded in closing the court.

This success prompted two Regulators, Job Shattuck and Oliver Parker, to plan another demonstration, this time against the Middlesex County courts. Several regiments of Regulators agreed to participate. But as the time for the demonstration approached, the Worcester County Regulators did not

ARMED REBELLION

show up, and the Bristol County Regulators sent word that, since the legislature had made an attempt to address their problems, they no longer wanted to close the courts. As a result, Shattuck and Parker abandoned their plan and the Middlesex courts were able to meet.

Two more conventions of disgruntled yeomen were held in the fall of 1786, this time in the eastern Massachusetts towns of Paxton and Concord. Governor James Bowdoin was alarmed that people in these towns, which were close to Boston, shared the same discontent with the government as western farmers. Topping the lists of grievances at the Concord and Paxton conventions was the fact that the legislature met in Boston. It was not just western farmers who resented having Boston as the state capital.

Governor Bowdoin began to fear that the rebellion in the west was spreading east. He asked United States Secretary at War Henry Knox to send troops from other states to help Massachusetts protect itself against Regulator uprisings. Knox asked the Confederation Congress to consider the request. Though they voted to raise more than thirteen hundred troops to help Massachusetts, the individual states were so short of cash and saddled with war debt that they were unable to supply soldiers for this army. Massachusetts was left to fend for itself.

Governor Bowdoin was not the only Massachusetts official concerned about the gathering momentum of the Regulators. General William Shepard, who commanded the Hampshire County

Henry Knox served as United States secretary of war under the Articles of Confederation. Knox was called upon by the governor of Massachusetts to provide assistance in dealing with the Regulators.

militia, had also written to Henry Knox, telling him that he feared the Regulators might launch an assault on the federal arsenal at Springfield. Shepard did not believe the Regulators wanted to achieve their goals through peaceful means. He told Knox, "I am surprised they have not seized the arsenal long before this time."[1] Another Massachusetts militia general, Benjamin Lincoln, a former Revolutionary War leader and a merchant wholesaler, wrote to his friend George Washington about the Regulator uprisings. Washington, who would later become the first president of the United States, wrote back, expressing his belief that a stronger national government was necessary to counteract the internal strife caused by groups such as the Regulators.

Lighthorsemen

After the legislature passed the Riot and Militia acts and suspended the writ of habeas corpus, bands of pro-government men began roaming the countryside, looking for the suspected leaders of the Regulators. Known as lighthorsemen, these men were armed and could be dangerous. The lighthorsemen were volunteers, mostly from Boston, and they traveled on horseback. They entered taverns and homes, looking for known Regulators. Some civilians were beaten by the lighthorsemen, especially if they did not cooperate by turning over suspects. The actions of the lighthorsemen outraged the country people and convinced them that the government was oppressive.

On the night of November 28, 1786, a volunteer unit of three hundred lighthorsemen from Boston, led by lawyer Benjamin Hitchbourn, rode out to Groton, Massachusetts, and attacked the houses of Regulators Job Shattuck, Oliver Parker, and Benjamin Page. Shattuck had long been associated with the Regulators. He had organized men to harass tax collectors as early as 1783. More recently, he had been involved in the plan to obstruct the Middlesex County courts. After this makeshift posse of lawyers, doctors, and merchants captured Shattuck and the other rebel leaders, they imprisoned the Regulators in Boston's Suffolk County jail. Job Shattuck, who had resisted capture, was seriously wounded with a broadsword wielded by one of the lighthorsemen.

As soon as the rebels were locked in the jail, word began to spread that other Regulators were planning to rescue the men. Boston lived in fear of an attack. Guards were positioned at the jail and at strategic points around Boston. Whether the Regulators wanted to free their men from jail or not, they never managed to do so. Some historians suggest that their attack on the Springfield arsenal in January 1787 may have been part of a larger plan among the Regulators to arm themselves effectively before marching to Boston to demand the release of these prisoners.

Lighthorsemen continued to terrorize civilians. On December 2, 1786, a group of lighthorsemen made up mostly of merchants and professionals from Worcester County raided the homes of Regulator supporters in Shrewsbury and injured several people. Soon, greatly exaggerated stories about the lighthorsemen began to spread throughout the countryside. One of the rumors said that Job Shattuck had been murdered at the hands of the lighthorsemen.

Yeoman farmers hated the lighthorsemen, and they feared future government attacks. "The seeds of war are now sown," two Shrewsbury yeomen announced after the attack by lighthorsemen. "Two of our men are now bleeding that were wounded by the lighthorse that came from Boston and Roxbury."[2]

Lighthorsemen made the Regulators fear the tyranny of the government even more. And growing numbers of Regulators began to compare the behavior of the Massachusetts government to that of Great

Britain before the Revolutionary War. Just as patriots had risen up to fight the tyranny of England, the Regulators began to think it might be necessary to overthrow the state. As one Regulator argued, "whenever any encroachments are made either upon the liberties or properties of the people, if redress [compensation] cannot be had without, it is virtue in them to disturb government."[3]

Organization Among the Regulators

As the year 1786 came to a close, and the state of Massachusetts began to pass oppressive legislation and fight back against the Regulators, the rebels grew stronger and more organized. From the beginning, the Regulators had been headed by Revolutionary War officers in the style of a militia. However, they were only loosely organized and there was no real centralization to their movement. Decisions were made by local leaders, who communicated with local leaders in other counties and towns.

Job Shattuck and Oliver Parker, both of whom were captured and jailed by lighthorsemen, had attempted the first broad-based demonstration of Regulators. In the fall of 1786, they had tried to involve many different groups of Regulators in a plan to obstruct the Middlesex courts, but this plan had failed. Now the Regulators tried to strengthen their organization.

On December 9, 1786, a committee of seventeen men was formed to act as captains among the regiments of Regulators. Daniel Shays was made captain of the Hampshire County Regulators. As a captain, one of his responsibilities was to enlist more men for the Regulator cause. He also had to be prepared to stop the courts from holding sessions whenever necessary.

On December 26, three hundred Regulators presented a united front when they once again prevented the courts from sitting in Springfield. The Regulators submitted a petition asking the judges not to hold court. This petition contained the signatures of Daniel Shays, Luke Day, and Thomas Grover. Shays himself

SOURCE DOCUMENT

Daniel Shays', Luke Day's, and Thomas Grover's names appeared on this petition given to the judges at the Springfield courthouse on December 26, 1786.

may not have been present, but because he had been a prominent figure at previous Regulator demonstrations, Thomas Grover signed Shays' name to the petition and Shays was associated with the event. From this point on, government officials considered Daniel Shays one of the most powerful leaders of the Regulators, even though Shays said he was not. In reality, the Regulators never had a very strong or effective leadership. They were primarily bands of like-minded men from different counties whose aim was to obstruct the courts. They were never able to achieve the kind of unity and strength necessary to present an effective opposition to the state.

Forming an Army to Fight the Regulators

Governor Bowdoin could not rely on the county militias to put down Regulator uprisings. Nor could he rely on the other states, since they had not been willing to provide funds to raise an army to help Massachusetts. Determined to create an army to fight the Regulators, Governor Bowdoin began doing his own fund-raising. As a merchant speculator, Bowdoin had many commercial ties. He now called on all of his friends and associates to contribute money to create and supply an army capable of opposing the western rebels and restoring order in Massachusetts. Many prominent merchants and wholesalers donated money to put this plan into action. Thousands of pounds were raised for the cause.

Former Revolutionary War General Benjamin Lincoln, who was also the first general of the Massachusetts militia, was chosen by Governor Bowdoin to lead this new army. The army, which consisted of approximately three thousand men, was made up of volunteers. Seven hundred African Americans from the Boston African Lodge of Masons, led by Prince Hall, had pledged their support to the government and offered to join Lincoln's army. Their offer was refused, probably because of their race. The army Governor Bowdoin raised consisted of volunteers from the merchant elite of the east coast, servants who had been sent to serve in their employers' places, and prominent professional and commercial men from inland market towns.

The new government troops formed five divisions, including two artillery regiments, and were furnished with muskets, bayonets, cartridge boxes, and thirty rounds of ammunition each. For provisions, they were given beef, bread, and rum. Called upon to serve for thirty days, it was agreed that each man would receive two pounds per month of service. Their orders were to protect the courts from any interference and to find and capture the Regulator leaders. On January 22, 1787, these government troops arrived in Worcester. They were ordered to guard the courthouse against any attempts by the Regulators to obstruct its proceedings. Their presence seemed to have an impact. At long last, the Worcester court held its scheduled sessions without interference.

The Regulators Plan Their Next Move

By the beginning of 1787, it was becoming harder and harder for the Regulators to function. In January, Governor Bowdoin had issued warrants for the arrest of sixteen Hampshire County Regulators, including Captain Daniel Shays. The warrants claimed that these men were dangerous to the safety and peace of Massachusetts. Soon four of these men were captured and arrested. The remaining twelve went into hiding. Daniel Shays had to keep bodyguards around him at all times. He worried about surprise attacks from lighthorsemen or from General Lincoln's army.

Now that Lincoln's army was trying to capture them, the Regulators had to improve the quality of their weapons in order to resist capture. They had never been well armed. In fact, some of the Regulators had only wooden clubs for protection. The Regulators were also short on supplies, and they did not always have enough food to eat when they marched to distant courthouses. These problems had to be solved.

In January 1787, Daniel Shays and four other Regulator captains circulated a letter among the different Regulator regiments. They asked the Regulators to muster, each man with ten days' worth of food and supplies, near Dr. Nehemiah Hind's tavern in Pelham by January 19.

When the Regulators had poured into Pelham, they discussed their next move. Two plans of action were considered. The Regulators wanted to launch an attack on the federal arsenal at Springfield. There, they could seize the weapons and ammunition they needed. They also wanted to negotiate the release of captured Regulators Job Shattuck, Oliver Parker, and Benjamin Page from jail in Boston.[4] Seizing weapons from the Springfield arsenal could be a first step toward a successful march on Boston, where they could secure the release of their prisoners. The Regulators also wanted to demonstrate in Boston. They were angry enough to launch an attack on the city. According to Shays, some of them wanted to "overthrow the present constitution."[5] Exactly what the Regulators had in mind is unclear, but they were willing to use force this time. They wanted to show the city of Boston how much they resented the policies of the state government.

Attack on the Springfield Arsenal

At the end of January 1787, the Regulators acted on the first half of their plan. They began to approach Springfield from all directions. Many of them marched through snow to assume their positions just outside the city. Badly in need of provisions, some of the regiments took food from shopkeepers as they passed by. They targeted shopkeepers who had harassed farmers and prosecuted them for debts.

Daniel Shays, with twelve hundred men from several counties, was stationed east of the arsenal in Palmer, while Eli Parsons, who led a regiment from Berkshire County, was at Chicopee with four hundred men. Captain Luke Day had four hundred men in West Springfield. Meanwhile, General William

Shepard and the remains of the Hampshire militia, numbering about one thousand men, were camped inside the Springfield arsenal, preparing to defend it against an attack.

As the groups of Regulators honed in on the arsenal from three directions, Shepard lost contact with the outside world. The Regulators, who had nearly surrounded the city of Springfield, were able to intercept most of the letters Shepard tried to send via messenger. They also tried to intercept all incoming messages. Fearing he might be outnumbered by Regulators, General Shepard had requested reinforcements. General Lincoln and his army of government troops were on their way to join him, but they were delayed by snowstorms.

Around 4:00 P.M. on the afternoon of January 25, General Shepard's scouts told him that Shays and his men were marching toward the arsenal. Absent were Luke Day and his regiment, who remained in West Springfield, unaware that their message asking the other captains to delay the attack had been intercepted by Shepard's men.

When Shays' regiment got within one hundred fifty yards of the arsenal, Shepard had his men fire the cannon twice over the rebels' heads. When they continued to march forward, they fired a third shot into their center as the column approached, killing four and wounding one. Shays' men scattered and some even deserted in the confusion that followed the cannon fire. Unable to retreat, lying dead and bleeding in the snow, were Regulators Ariel Webster and Ezekiel Root of Gill, John Hunter of Shelburne, and Jabez Spicer of Leyden. Another Regulator, Jeremiah McMillen of Pelham, had been wounded but had been taken off the battlefield.

Immediately following the bloodshed at the arsenal, those soldiers who remained under Daniel Shays' command retreated toward Ludlow. The next day, Shays and his men joined Eli Parsons and the Berkshire Regulators in Chicopee. They contemplated another attack on the arsenal. General Lincoln's arrival on January 27, however, prevented them from attempting another attack. Instead, they retreated toward Pelham.

Pursuing the Regulators

As soon as General Lincoln's army heard news of the conflict at the Springfield arsenal, they began pursuing the retreating Regulators. They crossed the Connecticut River on the ice in pursuit of Luke Day's men, who, upon hearing of the battle, had fled for Northampton. On January 28, Lincoln's army began chasing Shays, along with the Regulator regiments from Berkshire, Worcester, Hampshire, and Middlesex counties, who were retreating with him.

Lincoln and his army marched all through the night after the Regulators, but they moved slowly because of deep snowdrifts. Shays and his men arrived in Amherst just ahead of General Lincoln, and kept moving toward Shays' hometown of Pelham. As they marched, some Regulators raided stores in Hampshire

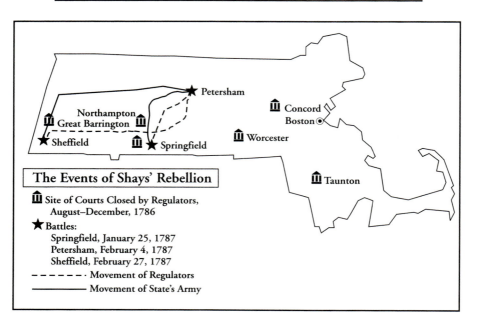

The events of Shays' Rebellion, including the Regulators' efforts to close down courts, can be seen on this map.

County. They harassed retailers they knew who had taken farmers to court. They also took food from their stores, since many of the Regulators lacked sufficient provisions.

Just after the rebels left Amherst for Pelham, ten sleigh loads of food and supplies arrived for them from Berkshire County. The sleigh drivers stopped to feed their horses at Oliver Clapp's tavern. Clapp happened to be a friend of Daniel Shays'. Knowing that Shays' men were in need of food, and aware that General Lincoln was not far behind, Clapp told the drivers not to stop but to press on for Pelham before they could be captured by Lincoln. Heeding his advice, the drivers continued on after the rebels, meeting them at Pelham. There, they were able to deliver the supplies, much to the relief of the Regulators. From January 28 to February 3, the Regulators camped at Pelham. Some of Shays' men camped on the common in front of the meetinghouse. Shays himself stayed at the old Conkey Tavern, while other men camped on East Hill, one of the highest points in Pelham.

Still chasing Shays, General Lincoln stopped at farmhouses from Amherst to Pelham, searching for Regulators. He found mostly women and children, because the majority of farmers in the area were with

Daniel Shays and the Regulators camped out by the Pelham meetinghouse during their retreat from General Benjamin Lincoln's forces.

the Regulators. Lincoln warned the women not to feed or house any Regulators. If they did so, they would be charged with treason against the state. But farm women in these towns supported the Regulator cause. According to several letters written by women from Pelham that were published in the *Massachusetts Gazette* in March 1787, Hampshire County women were enraged by the presence of General Lincoln and his army. They were outraged by the way General Lincoln's troops harassed them and searched their houses for Regulators. In some houses, the government troops had demanded that pro-Regulator women provide them with food and shelter. Hampshire County women were not the only ones who supported the Regulators. In the spring of 1787 when a group of merchants arrived in the southeastern town of Sharon, Massachusetts, to arrest men who had been prominent recruiters for the Regulators, they were heckled and harassed by a group of Regulators' wives and daughters, who called themselves "Shays women."[6]

On January 30, 1787, General Lincoln, who had camped with his army in Hadley, sent a letter to Daniel Shays, asking for his surrender. Shays and his men did not want to surrender unless they were guaranteed a pardon from the state. Otherwise, they might face the death penalty for their crimes against Massachusetts. Hoping to find some way out of their situation, they had already submitted a petition to the legislature, asking for pardon. Now Captain Shays sent a response to

General Lincoln, writing, ". . . the people are willing to lay down their arms, on the condition of a general pardon, and return to their respective homes, as they are unwilling to stain the land, which we in the late war purchased at so dear a rate, with the blood of our brethren and neighbors."[7] Lincoln sent word back that it was beyond his power to halt his mission. Unless the rebels surrendered at once, he would be forced to continue his pursuit.

General Lincoln also sent out scouts to spy on the Regulator camp in Pelham. Some of Shays' men may have seen them, because they decided not to wait for word from the legislature. Afraid of being captured by Lincoln's men, they packed up and marched to Petersham on February 8.

Petersham was only thirty miles from Pelham, but they thought they would be safe there because a heavy snow had fallen, making travel extremely difficult. However, as soon as Lincoln heard that Shays had left Pelham, he forced his army to pursue, snow or no snow. Lincoln's army marched the thirty miles to Petersham in deep snowdrifts that reached to their knees. Some of the men suffered frostbite. But Lincoln's army arrived in Petersham the next morning and surprised the Regulators. Shays and his men had only a few minutes' notice with which to grab their things and flee. General Lincoln's surprise attack dispersed Shays' forces, who scattered in all directions. Some fled with Shays toward Athol, in north-central

Old Church Petersham
Built-in-1784 | Removed-in-1842

General Lincoln's forces surprise-attacked Shays and his men while they were camped here in Petersham.

Massachusetts. Others fled in the direction of their homes. Some were captured by Lincoln's forces.

Having broken up Shays' ranks, General Lincoln and his men marched back to western Massachusetts to eliminate any remaining bands of rebels there. Regulators continued to gather at a few places in Berkshire County, including Lee, where two hundred fifty Regulators tried to prevent the courts from holding sessions in February 1787. Skirmishes between Regulators and the government continued in Berkshire County.

On the night of February 26, one hundred Regulators under the command of Captain Perez

Hamlin descended on Stockbridge, Massachusetts, pillaging homes and capturing several prominent citizens, whom they took as hostages. The Regulators were opposed by groups of state militiamen, and a brief battle occurred in Sheffield, Massachusetts, on February 27. Thirty Regulators were wounded and two were killed. Three pro-government men were killed and dozens wounded. It was the last battle of Shays' Rebellion.

Impact on the Legislature

The Regulators had long asked for reform, and through their actions they did eventually achieve some. Immediately following the uprisings of 1787, the Massachusetts legislature, at long last, responded to some of the demands of yeoman farmers. It passed laws that reduced lawyers' fees and created new registries of deeds in the western counties, making it easier for citizens there to conduct legal business. The legislature also voted to reduce the governor's salary, although the governor later vetoed this proposal. The tender law was also extended, and debtors were allowed to leave debtor's prison if they swore an oath saying that they had no property to pay their debts or sustain themselves while they were in prison. Taxes were lower in 1788 than they had been in eight years, and in future years the commercial classes were asked to contribute more. Though the new state legislature of 1787 did not address all the Regulators' concerns, it made positive changes that helped yeoman farmers.

Fate of the Rebels

By March 1787, most of the Regulators had fled Massachusetts. As many as two thousand went to Vermont and New York, sometimes bringing their families, their goods, and their livestock with them, despite an order that had been issued for the arrest of any Regulators who attempted to leave Massachusetts.

Though many Regulators fled the state, they continued to cause trouble in Massachusetts. In April 1787, while General Lincoln was soaking in the hot springs at New Lebanon, Massachusetts, he got word that one hundred twenty armed rebels from New York were descending upon him. The general escaped with just a few minutes to spare. General William Shepard, who had fired upon the Regulators at the Springfield arsenal in January, also continued to be harassed by the Regulators. He received death threats, his land was burned, and his horses were killed by Regulators seeking revenge.

Captains Daniel Shays, Luke Day, and Reuben Dickinson, along with many other Regulator leaders, sought refuge in Vermont. Some, like Reuben Dickinson, moved their families to unsettled territory in Vermont and began farming there. Regulators who moved to unsettled territory in Vermont, New Hampshire, and New York were able to start over.

A special court was created to try those Regulators who had been captured, such as Captain Jason Parmenter of the Hampshire County Regulators. During April and May 1787 this court held hearings.

Commonwealth of Maffachufetts.

By His EXCELLENCY

JamesBowdoin,Efq.

GOVERNOUR of the COMMONWEALTH of

MASSACHUSETTS.

A Proclamation.

WHEREAS by an Act paffed the fixteenth of February inftant, entitled, " An Act defcribing the difqualifications, to which perfons fhall be fubjected, which have been, or may be guilty of Treafon, or giving aid or fupport to the prefent Rebellion, and to whom a pardon may be extended," the General Court have eftablifhed and made known the conditions and difqualifications, upon which pardon and indemnity to certain offenders, defcribed in the faid Act, fhall be offered and given ; and have authorized and empowered the Governour, in the name of the General Court, to premife to fuch offenders fuch conditional pardon and indemnity :

I HAVE thought fit, by virtue of the authority vefted in me by the faid Act, to iffue this Proclamation, hereby premifing pardon and indemnity to all offenders within the defcription alorefaid, who are citizens of this State ; under fuch reftrictions, conditions and difqualifications, as are mentioned in the faid Act : provided they comply with the terms and conditions thereof, on or before the twenty-firft day of March next.

GIVEN at the Council Chamber in Bofton, this Seventeenth Day of February, in the Year of our LORD One Thoufand Seven Hundred and Eighty-Seven, and in the Eleventh Year of the Independence of the United States of AMERICA.

JAMES BOWDOIN.

By His Excellency's Command,
JOHN AVERY, jun. Secretary.

In this broadside of February 17, 1787, Governor Bowdoin offered pardons to the Regulators.

Many Regulators and Regulator sympathizers were pardoned. Some were fined and given jail sentences. Twelve men, Captain Parmenter among them, were convicted of treason and sentenced to death. On the day of their hangings, after the nooses had already been placed around their necks, they were granted a last-minute pardon from the state.

In Connecticut, Vermont, New Hampshire, and New York, officials cooperated with Massachusetts and tried to turn over suspected Regulators who were living within their borders. Many Regulators surrendered to the Massachusetts authorities, seeking forgiveness. Most were pardoned, provided that they agreed to sign an oath of allegiance to the state. Those who surrendered were barred from voting or holding elected office for three years. To prevent them from encouraging another rebellion, they were also disqualified from teaching school or running taverns. In some Massachusetts towns, so many men had been Regulators that there was no longer anyone in the whole town eligible to run for elected office. Not all state officials agreed with the way the Regulators were treated. Some, including General Lincoln, felt that disqualifying the Regulators from voting or holding public office was unfair. Others felt the state had been too lenient on the insurgents.

Daniel Shays After the Rebellion

Warrants had been issued for the arrest of Regulator leaders such as Daniel Shays, Luke Day, Adam

To obtain a pardon, most Regulators were required to sign an oath of allegiance to the state.

Wheeler, and Eli Parsons. A reward was offered for their arrest and return to Massachusetts. These men fled the state and remained in hiding.

Shays allegedly hid first in Vermont. He seemed to disappear completely, but he may still have been in touch with people in Pelham. Whether his wife, Abigail, fled with him is not known, but Shays later remarried. Legends began to develop about Daniel Shays. Some of these stories said that he had gone west into the wilderness. Others said that he had returned to Pelham briefly before leaving for Canada. Though Governor James Bowdoin had offered 150 pounds for his capture, Daniel Shays managed to elude authorities. He was never captured.

In February 1788, one year after the rebellion, he, or possibly his friends, petitioned for his pardon.

Captain Daniel Shays, who never considered himself the leader of the Regulators, lived the rest of his life in New York.

Shays was eventually granted a pardon from the state of Massachusetts in the summer of 1789. Shays did not return to Massachusetts, however. He lived out his days in the small town of Sparta, New York, where he might have gone unremembered if he had not met fourteen-year-old Millard Fillmore, who would one day become president of the United States.

Fillmore had arrived in Cayuga County, New York, to work as an apprentice in a wool-carding mill, where raw wool was processed into batting that could be spun into cloth. Fillmore lived next door to Daniel Shays, and they became friends. Fillmore enjoyed listening to the tales Shays told about his time in the army and with the Regulators. Fillmore, however, had difficulty imagining the Shays he knew as the Daniel Shays whose name was so prominently featured in the rebellion. He later wrote, "I remember Shays as a rather short, stout, unattractive man, and was always puzzled to understand how a man of such unattractive demeanor and so apparently retiring had ever been such a leader of men."[8]

While living in New York, Shays married a woman named Rhoda, the widow of a tavern keeper in Sparta, who had two grown sons. In 1820, Shays applied for a military pension based on his service during the Revolutionary War. He received it. After his pension came, he bought a small farm and built a house and barn, living out his days as a farmer. Daniel Shays died in Sparta, New York, on September 29, 1825, at the age of seventy-eight.

THE IMPACT OF SHAYS' REBELLION

The confrontation at the Springfield arsenal in January 1787 was the high point in a series of yeoman protests and Regulator conflicts that became known to history as Shays' Rebellion. Today, historians recognize that the Regulator movement was much larger than Daniel Shays himself. But the term *Shays' Rebellion* stuck, and it is still used today to describe the Regulator uprisings.

To eighteenth-century Americans, Shays' Rebellion evoked the fear that the new republic was falling apart. The United States was a young nation, a loose confederation of states, and now it seemed as though internal conflicts might tear it apart. Massachusetts had endured the most dramatic and violent uprisings, but many other states had also experienced rural uprisings over debt and taxes. During the 1780s, mobs in New Jersey, Maryland, New York, Pennsylvania, South Carolina, and Virginia all protested debtor courts and attacked tax collectors. Anarchy threatened to undermine the fledgling nation everywhere. Americans had fought hard for their independence, and they were determined not to let their country fall prey to internal strife and civil war. Many people wanted to take steps to make sure that events such as Shays' Rebellion would not happen again.

A Debate on National Government

Men such as James Madison, George Washington, and Alexander Hamilton had long argued that the Articles of Confederation, the governing document created by the Continental Congress toward the end of the American Revolution, was inadequate. They believed it needed to be revised to give more power to the federal government. After Shays' Rebellion, they became even more convinced that the national government needed to be stronger in order to prevent the governments of the states from falling apart.

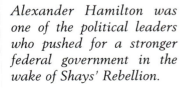

Alexander Hamilton was one of the political leaders who pushed for a stronger federal government in the wake of Shays' Rebellion.

George Washington reflected on Shays' Rebellion, writing that there was no "stronger evidence . . . of the want of energy in our governments than these disorders."[1] The Confederation's Secretary at War Henry Knox hoped that Shays' Rebellion would assist the Federalist cause by leading to the establishment of a stronger national government. (Federalists, as opposed to Anti-Federalists, believed in a strong central government, which, in some cases, would be stronger than the state governments.) Knox wrote that Shays' Rebellion had caused "changes in the minds of men in that state respecting the powers of government— everybody says they must be strengthened and that unless this shall be effected, there is no security for liberty and property."[2] Many Americans were now convinced that the federal government had to be strengthened. "I never saw so great a change in the public mind on any occasion as has lately appeared in this state as to the expediency of increasing the powers of Congress, not merely to commercial objects but generally," wrote one Massachusetts man.[3]

Only one major American political thinker was not concerned about Shays' Rebellion. Thomas Jefferson, author of the Declaration of Independence, was serving as the American ambassador to France when he heard of the uprisings in Massachusetts. Unlike other political leaders, Jefferson argued that Shays' Rebellion was a useful and educational event. "What country can preserve its liberties," he wrote from Paris, if its rulers are not warned from time to time that their people preserve the spirit of resistance? What signify a few lives lost in a century or two? The tree of liberty must be refreshed from time to time, with the blood of patriots and tyrants. It is its natural manure.[4]

Jefferson also told his friend James Madison that he thought rebellions were "a medicine necessary for the sound health of government."[5] Without them, governments might become corrupt.

Revising the Articles of Confederation

The Regulator uprisings in Massachusetts had drawn attention to some of the problems with the Articles of Confederation. Had the Confederation government been stronger, statesmen argued, it might have been able to avert the crises in Massachusetts. For example, if the national government had been able to set monetary policy or take steps to help solve the financial crises of the 1780s, Shays' Rebellion might never have happened. If the Confederation had been able to help Massachusetts put down the Regulator movement, events might have taken a different turn. Though the Confederation government had tried to raise an army to help Massachusetts, the individual states had not followed through with the funding they promised. Since the national government did not have the power to tax, it had no money itself. As a result, it was powerless to act on behalf of the states.

A May 1787 meeting of the Continental Congress had already been called before the confrontation at the Springfield arsenal in January, but the violence in

Massachusetts increased attendance at this convention. Many delegates attended who otherwise might not have, because they were shocked by the uprisings in Massachusetts and afraid that the same thing might happen in their own states.

Fifty-five delegates from twelve states—every state except Rhode Island—attended the 1787 Constitutional Convention in Philadelphia. James Madison of Virginia had drafted a plan of government, which the Virginia delegation adopted and presented to the convention. Madison's plan took into account problems with the Confederation government, such as the lack of cooperation between states and the ways in which the states infringed upon the authority of the national government. Madison believed that the national government should not be subject to the power of any one state or interest group. He recommended a system of checks and balances that would prevent any one group from gaining control.

James Madison was the primary architect of the United States Constitution.

The delegates met behind closed doors and deliberated in secret, discussing their business only among themselves. They had a lot to consider. Over many issues, such as slavery and representation in the national, or federal, legislature, there was intense disagreement. Delegates debated the ways in which the states could be represented in the federal government and how political power could be distributed equally among three different branches of national government—legislative, executive, and judicial—so that each branch would check the power of the others.

With Shays' Rebellion in mind, delegates also discussed the need for a national army that could be called upon to put down insurrections. Delegates voted to give the federal government more power to suppress rebellions. Elbridge Gerry, one of the Massachusetts delegates to the convention, also had Shays' Rebellion in mind when he argued that "the evils we experience flow from the excess of democracy."[6] Gerry warned delegates that the people of a state were easily misled and that this fact should be considered before they decided to allow the people themselves, rather than members of the state governments, to elect representatives directly to the national legislature.

When they were finished, the delegates had not just revised the Articles of Confederation. They had created a whole new constitution. Not everyone was happy with the new document. Three delegates, including George Mason and Patrick Henry of Virginia, felt that too many of the states' rights had

At Independence Hall in Philadelphia, the Continental Congress met to create the new United States Constitution.

been taken away and that the constitution needed a bill of rights to protect individuals from the excesses of federal power. They refused to sign the final document. In September 1787, the delegates sent the constitution to the individual states for ratification, or approval. At least nine states needed to ratify the Constitution before it could be adopted.

Anti-Federalists Versus Federalists in Massachusetts

Voters in each state elected delegates to attend state conventions, where they would decide whether to accept the new constitution. In Massachusetts, as elsewhere, people sided with one of two camps—the Anti-Federalists and the Federalists. Anti-Federalists opposed the new constitution because it took power away from the states and lacked a bill of rights. Most Regulators and Shays' Rebellion sympathizers were Anti-Federalists. They feared that, by giving more power to the federal government, the power of the states would be threatened. They also worried that, if the federal Congress had the power to tax, they would face higher taxes. Federalists, many of whom were merchants and professionals, supported the new Constitution. They had long argued that the national government ought to have greater power. They wanted uniform trade policies, and in order to get them, Congress had to have the power to coordinate the actions of all the states.

Amos Singletary was among the delegates to the Massachusetts state convention who opposed the new constitution. In a speech to the convention, he expressed the fears of many of the state's small farmers, arguing that men of wealth would use federal power to control all men. "These lawyers, and men of learning, and moneyed men, that talk so finely, and gloss over matters so smoothly, to make us poor illiterate people swallow down the pill, expect to get into Congress themselves," Singletary said.

> [T]hey expect to be the managers of this Constitution, and get all the power and all the money into their own hands, and then they will swallow up all us little folks, like the great *Leviathan*, Mr. President; yes, just as the whale swallowed up *Jonah*. That is what I am afraid of. . . .[7]

There were some Massachusetts farmers who supported the new constitution, however, in the hope that it might ensure peace. Farmer Jonathan Smith was among the delegates to the Massachusetts ratification convention. He told the other delegates,

> I have lived in a part of the country where I have known the worth of good government by the want of it. There was a black cloud that rose in the east last winter, and spread over the west. . . . It brought on a state of anarchy, and that led to tyranny. . . . People that used to live peaceably, and were before good neighbors, got distracted, and took up arms against government. . . . Now, Mr. President, when I saw this Constitution, I found that it was a cure for these disorders. It was just such a thing as we wanted.[8]

In the end, the Federalists won the ratification debate in Massachusetts. By a vote of 187 to 168, Massachusetts approved the new constitution in 1788. The dividing lines were nearly the same as they had been in opinion about Shays' Rebellion. The chief opponents of ratification were delegates from western Massachusetts, where the Regulators had been most active. Likewise, most of the delegates who approved the new constitution were from eastern seaboard commercial centers and market towns.

By the summer of 1788, the Constitution had been ratified by nine states and was officially adopted as the new governing document for the United States. Shays' Rebellion had played a vital role in the creation of the United States Constitution. The fear the rebellion had evoked helped the Federalists in their crusade for a

Daniel Shays and the Regulators are still remembered for their role in the decision to draft the United States Constitution. This memorial to the Regulators was erected by the town of Pelham.

stronger government. As shown by the preamble to the new Constitution, Americans hoped to "insure domestic tranquility" by establishing the Constitution of the United States.[9] The memory of Shays' Rebellion and the fear of other possible rebellions pushed many people who might otherwise have rejected a stronger national government to accept one.

★ TIMELINE ★

1747—Daniel Shays is born in Hopkington, Massachusetts.

1760s—Upset over high taxes and a lack of representation,
–1770s farmers calling themselves Regulators rise up against the Carolina governments.

1775—Battles of Lexington and Concord begin the Revolutionary War; Daniel Shays joins a company of minutemen and responds to the Lexington alarm.

1780—Massachusetts adopts the first state constitution.

1781—Americans defeat the British at the Battle of Yorktown; Massachusetts is awash in war debt; Massachusetts levies an unpopular excise in order to raise revenue.
February 11: A convention of yeomen meets at Hadley, Massachusetts, to discuss its grievances with the state government.
February 26: A mob of three hundred yeomen attempts to obstruct the proceedings of the debtor court in Pittsfield.
April: Debtor Samuel Ely instigates an attack on the Hampshire County debtor court in Northampton.
April 9: Twenty-six Worcester County towns send delegates to a Worcester convention, where they discuss their fiscal woes.

1783—The Treaty of Paris officially ends the Revolutionary War.
May 27: Hampshire County yeomen gather to prevent the courts from sitting at Springfield.

1785—Citizens in Maine begin agitating for separation from Massachusetts.

1786—Fifty towns in Hampshire County send delegates to the Hatfield Convention to discuss their grievances; Fifteen hundred armed men, led by Regulators Luke Day, Joseph Hinds, and Joel Billings, obstruct the debtor court in Northampton.

September: Regulators obstruct the courts in Worcester.

September 23–27: Regulator Captains Daniel Shays and Luke Day lead a demonstration at the Springfield courthouse, where the Supreme Judicial Court had convened to rule on the activities of the Regulators.

November: The state legislature ends its session after passing the Riot and Militia acts, designed to crush the Regulator rebellion.

November 28: Three hundred lighthorsemen from Boston attack the houses of Regulators Job Shattuck, Oliver Parker, and Benjamin Page, capturing the men and imprisoning them in Boston.

December 2: Lighthorsemen from Worcester County conduct raids on the homes of Regulator sympathizers in Shrewsbury, injuring several people in the process.

December 4: General Lincoln sends a letter to George Washington, warning him of the conflicts in Massachusetts; Washington is perturbed by the actions of the Regulators.

December 9: The Regulators elect a "committee of seventeen" to act as captains among their regiments; Daniel Shays is chosen to lead a group of Hampshire County Regulators.

December 20: General William Shepard, head of the Worcester County militia, writes to Secretary at War Henry Knox, expressing his concern about the possibility of a Regulator attack on the Springfield arsenal.

December 26: Three hundred Regulators obstruct the courts in Springfield.

1787—*January*: Massachusetts Governor James Bowdoin raises an army of three thousand men to fight the Regulators; Warrants are issued for the arrest of the Regulator leaders.

January 19: At Daniel Shays' request, the Regulator regiments muster in Pelham, where they draw up plans for an attack on the federal arsenal at Springfield.

January 22: Governor Bowdoin's army, led by General Lincoln, arrives in Worcester, Massachusetts, to protect the courts and capture Regulator leaders.

January 25: Regulators from Hampshire, Berkshire, Worcester, Bristol, Middlesex, and Suffolk counties attempt an attack on the Springfield arsenal; General William Shepard orders the state militiamen to fire at the rebels; Four Regulators are killed.

January 28: General Lincoln's army pursues Daniel Shays and the retreating Regulators as they head toward Pelham, Massachusetts.

January 30: Shays writes to the legislature, agreeing to surrender if the state will pardon the Regulators.

February 8: General Lincoln's forces surprise the Regulators in Petersham, forcing them to scatter; Many Regulators flee the state for Vermont, New York, or Canada.

February 26: Berkshire Regulators led by Perez Hamlin battle state militiamen in Sheffield, Massachusetts; Thirty Regulators are wounded and two killed.

March: The Massachusetts legislature enacts debtor relief laws and reforms.

May: The Continental Congress convenes in Philadelphia to revise the Articles of Confederation.

September: The Continental Congress sends the United States Constitution to the states for ratification.

1788— The United States Constitution is formally adopted.

1789— Daniel Shays is granted a pardon by the state of Massachusetts.

1820— Daniel Shays receives a United States military pension for his service during the Revolutionary War.

1825— Daniel Shays dies in Sparta, New York, at the age of seventy-eight.

★ CHAPTER NOTES ★

Chapter 1. A Violent Uprising

1. Mary Beth Norton et al., *A People and a Nation*, 3rd ed. (Boston: Houghton Mifflin, 1990), vol. 1, p. 157.

2. David P. Szatmary, *Shays' Rebellion: The Making of an Agrarian Insurrection* (Amherst: University of Massachusetts Press, 1980), p. 102.

3. Martin Kaufman, ed., *Shays' Rebellion: Selected Essays* (Westfield, Mass.: Westfield State College, 1987), p. 17.

Chapter 2. Life After the Revolution

1. George Richards Minot, *History of the Insurrections in Massachusetts in 1786* (New York: Da Capo Press, 1971), p. 6.

2. Mary Beth Norton et al., *A People and a Nation*, 3rd ed. (Boston: Houghton Mifflin, 1990), vol. 1, p. 171.

3. Robert J. Taylor, *Western Massachusetts in the Revolution* (Providence, R.I.: Brown University Press, 1954), p. 106.

4. David P. Szatmary, *Shays' Rebellion: The Making of an Agrarian Insurrection* (Amherst: University of Massachusetts Press, 1980), p. 1.

5. Ibid., p. 2.

6. Gloria L. Main, "The Distribution of Consumer Goods in Colonial New England," *Early American Probate Inventories*, ed. Peter Benes (Boston: Boston University Press, 1987), p. 161.

7. T. H. Breen, "An Empire of Goods," *Colonial America*, eds. Stanley Katz et al. (New York: McGraw-Hill, 1993), p. 389.

8. Szatmary, p. 25.

9. Robert A. Gross, ed., *In Debt to Shays: The Bicentennial of an Agrarian Rebellion* (Charlottesville: University Press of Virginia, 1993), p. 299.

10. Martin Kaufman, ed., *Shays' Rebellion: Selected Essays* (Westfield, Mass.: Westfield State College, 1987), p. 6.

11. Ibid., pp. 5–6.

12. John H. Lockwood, ed., *Western Massachusetts: A History 1636–1925* (New York: Lewis Historical Publishing Co., 1926), vol. 1, p. 127.

13. Szatmary, p. 33.

14. Ibid., pp. 33–34.

15. Taylor, p. 111.

16. Szatmary, p. 34.

17. Taylor, p. 133.

18. Ibid., p. 109.

19. Ibid.

20. Szatmary, p. 41.

Chapter 3. Petitions and Protest

1. Robert J. Taylor, *Western Massachusetts in the Revolution* (Providence, R.I.: Brown University Press, 1954), p. 135.

2. David P. Szatmary, *Shays' Rebellion: The Making of an Agrarian Insurrection* (Amherst: University of Massachusetts Press, 1980), p. 47.

3. C. O. Parmenter, *History of Pelham, Mass., 1738–1898* (Amherst: Carpenter and Morehouse, 1898), pp. 389–390.

4. Szatmary, p. 63.

5. Gordon Wood, *The Creation of the American Republic, 1776–1787* (Chapel Hill: University of North Carolina Press, 1969), p. 327.

6. Szatmary, p. 83.

7. Wood, p. 326.

Chapter 4. Armed Rebellion

1. David P. Szatmary, *Shays' Rebellion: The Making of an Agrarian Insurrection* (Amherst: University of Massachusetts Press, 1980), p. 99.

2. Ibid., p. 94.

3. Mary Beth Norton et al., *A People and a Nation*, 3rd ed. (Boston: Houghton Mifflin, 1990), vol. 1, p. 158.

4. John H. Lockwood, ed., *Western Massachusetts: A History 1636–1925* (New York: Lewis Historical Publishing Co., 1926), vol. 1, p. 157.

5. Szatmary, p. 100.

6. Ibid., p. 117.

7. C. O. Parmenter, *History of Pelham, Mass., 1738–1898* (Amherst, Mass.: Carpenter and Morehouse, 1898), pp. 379–380.

8. Mabel Cook Coolidge, *The History of Petersham, Massachusetts* (Hudson, Mass.: Powell Press, 1948), p. 129.

Chapter 5. The Impact of Shays' Rebellion

1. David P. Szatmary, *Shays' Rebellion: The Making of an Agrarian Insurrection* (Amherst: University of Massachusetts Press, 1980), p. 123.

2. Ibid., p. 127.

3. Robert A. Gross, ed., *In Debt to Shays: The Bicentennial of an Agrarian Rebellion* (Charlottesville: University Press of Virginia, 1993), p. 116.

4. Mary Beth Norton et al., *A People and a Nation,* 3rd ed. (Boston: Houghton Mifflin, 1990), vol. 1, p. 176.

5. Thomas A. Bailey and David M. Kennedy, *The American Spirit*, 6th ed. (Lexington, Mass.: D.C. Heath and Co., 1987), vol. 1, p. 130.

6. Ibid., pp. 130–131.

7. Jonathan Elliot, *The Debates in the Several State Conventions, on the Adoption of the Federal Constitution*, 2nd ed. (Washington: 1836), vol. 2, p. 102.

8. Ibid., pp. 102–103.

9. Preamble to the United States Constitution.

★ Further Reading ★

Books

Collier, Christopher, and James L. Collier. *Creating the Constitution*. Tarrytown, N.Y.: Marshall Cavendish Corporation, 1998.

Greene, Jack. *Colonies to Nation 1763–1789*. New York: Norton, 1975.

Gross, Robert A., ed. *In Debt to Shays: The Bicentennial of an Agrarian Rebellion*. Charlottesville: University Press of Virginia, 1993.

Kaufman, Martin, ed. *Shays' Rebellion: Selected Essays*. Westfield, Mass.: Westfield State College Institute for Massachusetts Studies, 1987.

Minot, George Richards. *History of the Insurrections in Massachusetts in 1786*. New York: Da Capo Press, 1971.

Nardo, Don, ed. *The American Revolution*. San Diego, Calif.: Greenhaven Press, 1998.

Szatmary, David P. *Shay's Rebellion: The Making of an Agrarian Insurrection*. Amherst: University of Massachusetts Press, 1980.

Internet Addresses

Massachusetts Historical and Governmental Sites. April 7, 1999. <http://www.hsu.edu/faculty/worthf/states/massachu.html> (August 12, 1999).

The Shay Group. *Shays Rebellion*. 1996. <http://www.shaysnet.com/~shayg/dshay.htm> (August 12, 1999).

Supreme Judicial Court Historical Society. *Shays' Rebellion*. 1998. <http://www.sjchs-history.org/shays.html> (August 12, 1999).

★ INDEX ★

DATE DUE

GAYLORD   PRINTED IN U.S.A.